THE
BOATS
—◇ OF ◇—
MEN-*of*-WAR

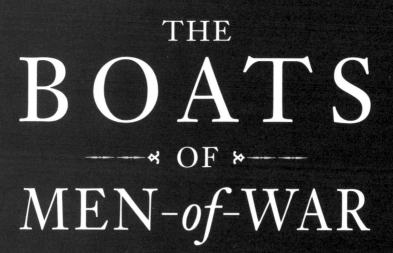

THE
BOATS
❖ OF ❖
MEN-*of*-WAR

Commander W E May

With additions by Simon Stephens

CAXTON EDITIONS

This edition first published in the United Kingdom by the National Maritime Museum
and Chatham Publishing, 61 Frith Street, London WIV 5TA

Chatham Publishing is an imprint of Gerald Duckworth & Co Ltd

This edition published 2003 by Caxton Editions an imprint of The Caxton Publishing Group

British Library Cataloguing in Publication Data
A catalogue record for this book is available from the British Library

ISBN I 84067 4318

Designed by Martin Richards, London

Printed in Dubai by Oriental Press

Frontispiece The boats of the British fleet actively employed against a French
fireship attack off Quebec, 28 June 1759. Oil painting by Dominic Serres
the elder. *(BHC0392)*

CONTENTS

PUBLISHERS' NOTE

This new edition preserves the late Commander May's original text and notes in their entirety, only obvious errors being corrected. The new material, assembled by Simon Stephens of the National Maritime Museum, comprises all the tabular data, the illustrations, and their captions.

FOREWORD

The author of this monograph, Commander W E May, was Deputy Director of the National Maritime Museum from 1951 to 1968. Although distinguished primarily as a specialist in the history of navigation, he expanded his knowledge of various aspects of this nation's maritime story to embrace a number of topics bearing on the social life of seamen. He has published works on the history of naval uniform, naval weapons and has been responsible for very many contributions to learned periodicals all of which have been concerned with detailed aspects of naval history.

One of his subjects has been the equipment of warships including their compasses and now their boats. This study is concerned with the various types of subsidiary vessel employed by warships of all types from the earliest days to the beginning of the twentieth century, from small boats and dinghies to steam pinnaces, many of which are illustrated here. He has drawn his information from many sources, published and unpublished and from the Museum's collection of draughts.

Basil Greenhill

Chapter 1 EARLY HISTORY

The earliest information which has come to hand concerning the boats carried by men-of-war is derived from the inventories of ships. The first of these to be noticed was reported by Nicolas,[1] but his work has to be accepted with caution for Moore[2] has pointed out that in one case at least he has been mistaken in his source and has dated it too early. Nicolas quotes the receipt of Thomas de Stetesham, clerk of the King's ship called *La George*, 1345-1346. The partial quotations which he gives imply that she had two boats, called respectively a 'long-boat' and a 'cockett', that each had six oars and that the former had in addition four long ones called 'skulles', and that one boat had a sail. The prices of the oars give a rough idea of the relative dimensions of the boats and were as follows:

For the larger boat	8d each
For the 'skulles'	½d each
For the 'cockett'	5d each

I am not too happy that Nicolas really found a boat called a longboat in these inventories and remain unconvinced that this nomenclature had been adopted at so early a date. All the same, it is necessary to record his findings until someone should have closely examined the original manuscript.[3]

Inventories of 1485-1495 show that a large ship then carried three boats. For example those of the *Sovereign* were called a 'Grete Bote', a 'Cokkebote' and a 'Bote called the jollyvatt'.[4] The relative sizes of these can be judged by the fact that the grete bote had eighteen oars, a 'Foreskolle' and an 'After skolle', the cokkebote had twelve oars and an 'After skully', while the jolly-vatt (soon after to be spelt jollywatt) had but four oars. The skolle, or skully, was probably shorter than an oar and was used by the bow and stroke oars-men, where the boat narrowed at bow and stern. Their use does not seem to have persisted very long. This appears to be in direct opposition to the long large oars called skullys, quoted by Nicolas. Each boat had a mast and a single sail. The two larger boats had each a yard, suggesting that while their sails were quadrilateral lug-sails that of the jollyvatt was triangular, and hence relatively smaller.

One of the principal duties of the two larger boats was to weigh or lay out anchors. To assist in this each had a davit with a sheave which was of iron in the grete bote and of brass for the cokkebote of the *Sovereign*. In addition the grete bote had a 'shyver of yron in the Botes head', which might at first suggest that the davit was fitted in the stern while the sheave in the bow was sometimes used as an alternative. Boteler however definitely states that the davit was fitted in the bow.[5] Anchors were provided for the grete bote and cokke. Another inventory refers to 'bote hokes'. 'Chaynes of yron in the bowes of the seid Bote' are mentioned in the *Regent's* inventory[6] and for the *Mary Fortune* we find 'a Chayne for the Botes Bow with ij loff hokes of yron weyng togeder xiiij lb price the lb j^d ob–xxj^d'[7] being purchased among other ironwork. It is not clear what these chains were for, unless they were for hoisting the boat.

The origin of the name 'grete bote' is obvious, but those of the other two are not. At first sight one might think that 'cokke' is derived from the French *coque*, but Jal[8] thinks that as *coque* originated in northern France rather than in the Mediterranean it is the other way round and that the French *coque* is derived from the English 'cokke', with a similar derivation to that of cog, the name of a medieval type of sailing vessel. A curious offshoot of cokke is the name coxswain, originally meaning the man who steered the cokke but very shortly changing to mean one who steered any ship or boat.

This convincingly detailed painting by van Wieringen is dated 1616 and shows an English privateer off La Rochelle. The size of the double-ended longboat in the foreground demonstrates how near-impossible it was to hoist in such large craft. (*BHC0723*)

'Jollyvatt' might also suggest a French origin through *jolie*, but no explanation would then appear for vatt or watt. On the other hand in modern German we have *jolle* for a small boat and *watt* meaning a shoal. Was the small jollywatt a little boat for use in shoal water? Again we are faced with the problem in which language the words appeared first.

Alan Moore has drawn attention to a third set of inventories dating from 1410–1412.[9] These throw very little light on boats. The inventories for the *Christophre* are in two parts, the 'Recept' and the 'liberatio', in which the entries roughly parallel each other. Thus in the first we have 'j batell cum ij mastes' and in the other 'j batell long'. These appear to indicate that the largest boat had now become known as the longboat and that she had two masts. She also had thirteen oars and two sculls.

Moore also gives the inventory for the *Carake*, which includes:

> ij barkes
> j gundard cum v ores

Previous pages Painted by Adam Willaerts in 1622, this depiction of the Elector Palatine embarking at Dover on 25 April 1613 shows the *Prince Royal* surrounded by boats, some under sail. The ship astern of the flagship has a large double-ended boat at her starboard quarter, while the *Prince* is attended by two long, narrow boats with small transoms, probably defined as barges. (*BHC0266*)

He suggests that 'barke' and 'gundard' are foreign types of boats, for the *Carake* had been purchased abroad. 'Barke' is of course *barca*, now used in Spanish for any type of ship's boat. There is no such word as gundard in any of the principal Mediterranean languages, but *guindar* in Spanish means to hoist and I suggest that the entry 'j gundard cum v ores' may be taken as applying to a boat's apparel and meaning that there were a davit and five oars on board for one of the *barcas*.

Below In this Abraham Willaerts painting of an unidentified engagement during the First Dutch War (1652-1654), English boats are much in evidence. One ship tows her longboat, while a large fourteen-oared boat in the foreground appears to be transferring a flag officer. (*BHC0823*)

ESTABLISHMENTS OF BOATS, 1600-1700

In 1618 a committee was appointed to investigate abuses in the Royal Navy.[10] One of the aspects of this enquiry was a census of boats carried by the ships and suggestions for modifications to the establishment for the future. It transpired that each ship of the first three rates should have been carrying three boats, a longboat, a pinnace and a skiff. Two points immediately appear: the cokkeboat of earlier times had given way to the pinnace and the jollywatt to the skiff. In the suggested new establishment the skiff once more gave place to the jollywatt. They may have been the same thing, though from the dimensions given the skiff was in general rather finer in her lines.

In the census, boats vary considerably in size. The First Rate *Prince* had a longboat of 52ft 4in length, just under half the length of her own keel which was 115ft. Even the Second Rate *Assurance* with a keel length of only 95ft carried a 51ft 3in longboat. The smallest was carried by the Third Rate *Speedwell*, her longboat being 40ft 6in and her own keel 84ft. The proposed establishment gave a longboat, pinnace and jollywatt to each First and Second Rate and a longboat and pinnace to each Third Rate. The 66ft *Desire*, which previously had had a skiff only was now to have a pinnace and no other boat. It was proposed that boats should be standardised at a few sizes and that longboats should be smaller. That for the *Prince* would be only 42ft long, that for the *Speedwell* 31ft while the smallest, for the *Adventure* and *Phoenix*, would be 28ft. Pinnaces which had varied between 30ft 8in and 19ft 8in would be standardised between 29ft and 26ft, and all jollywatts would be 20ft, replacing skiffs from 19ft 8in to 17ft 6in. The proportions of length to breadth for the new boats are interesting. The lengths of longboats were to be 3.8 times the breadth for the largest boats to 3.5 times for the smallest. For pinnaces the proportion varied from 4 to 3.8 times, and for the jollywatt it was only 3.1 times. Some of the older longboats had been finer even than the pinnaces and the skiffs were finer than the jollywatts. One unusual boat was present when the census was taken: the *Prince* had a shallop instead of the skiff. This boat was 27ft 8in long and its length was 4.2 times its breadth.

In 1627 orders were given for a survey to be made of the boats of all the ships at Chatham.[11] It is evident that little had been done to implement the proposals of nine years before. longboats with lengths of up to 52ft were still in evidence, while the variations in dimensions of the jollywatts suggests that the boats so-called were often in fact the skiffs of the earlier census.

The great length of the longboats made it difficult, if not almost impossible to hoist them in and for this reason they were often towed while on passage or even left behind. In 1625 the Cadiz fleet lost every one of its

During the fleet battles of the Dutch Wars the boats of both sides were often actively involved in their own small fights. Boats were needed to take off the crews of fireships as they were abandoned to drift down on the enemy. Conversely, boats were used to board or tow off the opposing fireships, and this often brought the boats and their crews into direct conflict, well demonstrated in the foreground of this Monamy painting of the burning of the *Royal James* at Solebay, 28 May 1672. (*BHC0301*)

longboats when crossing the Bay of Biscay.[12] Sir Henry Mainwaring, who is believed to have written about 1625 although his dictionary was not published until 1644, implies that the longboat was never hoisted. He says:

> A good longboat will live in any grown sea if the water be sometimes freed, unless the sea breaks very much. The rope by which it is towed at the ship's stern is called the boat rope, to which, to keep the boat from sheering, we add another, which we call a guest-rope. We do also to save the bows of the boat, which would be torn out with the twitches which the ship under sail would give, use to swift her, that is, take fast a rope round the gunwale, and to that make fast the boat rope.[13]

On the other hand Nathaniel Boteler describes the longboat as 'the biggest of Boats that may, and are hoised in, into the Ship,' [14] making it quite clear that it was expected that she could be hoisted in.

Certainly by the middle of the century some ships were hoisting in their longboats on occasion. Sir Thomas Allin refers to hoisting out the longboat of the *Plymouth* (60) on the 10 January 1660/1.[15] The log of the *Phoenix* (42 guns), when on her voyage to India in 1684-1687, refers on more than one occasion to having towed her longboat for several days after proceeding to sea, before hoisting it.[16] One would have thought that if the longboat were to be hoisted in the end it would have been more convenient to do so while still in harbour. In May 1697 Vice-Admiral Neville with a squadron of nine ships chased a French squadron under M de Pointis in the West Indies. The English ships were towing their longboats and all but two cut them adrift in an effort to increase their speed so that they might come up with the enemy. The loss of all these boats caused great inconvenience when the ships had to water later. [17]

The report on boats in 1627 mentions five types of boats, their lengths being:

Longboats	between 52ft 0in and 21ft 3in
Barge	36ft 9in
Pinnaces	between 32ft 4in and 25ft 0in
Shallop	27ft
Jollywatts	between 20ft and 14ft

Only one ship, the *Red Lyon*, had a barge and she had a pinnace and a jollywatt in addition, but no longboat. Only the *Prince*, now known as the *Prince Royal* (55 guns), still had her shallop, accompanied by a longboat and a jollywatt.

The Length, Breadth, and Depth of Boates Belonging to His Majestie's Ships', about 1640

		Length Feet-ins	Breadth Feet-ins	Depth Feet-ins
Soveraigne	Longboat	50-10	12-6	4-3
	Pinnace	36-0	9-6	3-3
	Skiff	27-0	7-0	3-0
Prince	Longboat	44-8	11-0	4-0
	Pinnace	34-0	7-0	3-1
	Skiff	25-0	6-6	2-9
Merhonour, Tryumph, James	Longboat	38-0	10-9	4-2
	Pinnace	31-0	6-8	3-0
	Skiff	24-0	6-3	2-6
2nd Ranke Ships	Longboat	35-0	9-6	3-7
	Pinnace	29-0	7-0	2-8
	Skiff	20-0	6-0	2-5
3rd Ranke Ships	Longboat	33-0	8-6	3-4
	Pinnace	28-0	7-2	3-0
4th Ranke Ships	Longboat	29-6	9-0	2-11
	Pinnace	22-0	6-0	2-3
5th Ranke Ships	Longboat	24-10	7-9	2-10

From G S Laird Clowes (ed), *The Lengths of Masts & Yards, etc,1640*, The Society for Nautical Research Occasional Publications No 1 (London 1931).

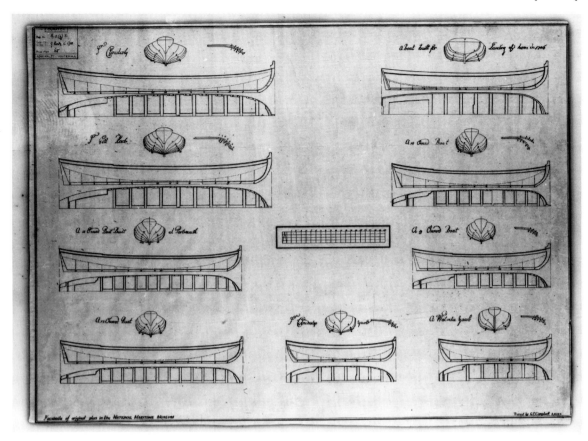

A tracing of a badly damaged original showing the form of nine typical boats of about 1700. From top left, reading down, they are: Sir Cloudisley Shovell's boat, a twenty-oared barge; Sir George Rooke's barge, also with twenty oars; a twelve-oared boat built at Portsmouth; another twelve-oared boat; Sir Cloudisley Shovell's yawl (centre); a boat built for landing men in 1706; a ten-oared boat; a nine-oared boat; a West India yawl. (*Bu(g)5*)

A 30ft ten-oared barge or pinnace shown on the booms (spare topmasts) of the Sixth Rate 20-gun *Tartar* of 1734 graphically demonstrates the problem of stowing boats aboard the smaller warships. If this were the establishment 27ft pinnace, then the *Tartar* would also have to find space for a 17ft Deal yawl. (*SLR0228/B1807*)

Chapter 2 TYPES OF BOATS

T he **barge** has become associated in recent times with the flag officer as his personal boat and indeed Blanckley[18] refers to it in 1750 as rowing twelve oars and being 'allowed to Flag Officers as Pinnaces are to Captains'. Sir R Massie Blomfield[19] quotes Sir Walter Raleigh as saying 'I had taken my Barge and gone ashore'[20] and assumes from this that the barge must have been Sir Walter's personal boat. I cannot agree that any such assumption is tenable for from passages in Raleigh's account of his earlier 1595 voyage it is clear to me that when he says 'my barge' he means the barge belonging to his ship.[21] This has always been quite common phraseology among sea officers.

The name *barge* is one of those irritating words in the English language which have a plurality of meanings – in this case five.

There are barges of sturdy and roomy build, intended for the carriage of quantities of cargo, and these are subdivided into two classes of quite different form: dumb barges which have to be towed and self-propelled barges, the latter originally proceeding under sail and now commonly fitted with motors.

A contemporary model of a heavily decorated 37ft barge of the first half of the eighteenth century, almost certainly a flag officer's boat. The boat has a beam of 7ft with twelve fixed rowlocks *en echelon* for single-banked rowing. In full-sized practice the chequered pattern would be provided by painted canvas over the bottom boards. (*SLR0333/D4052C*)

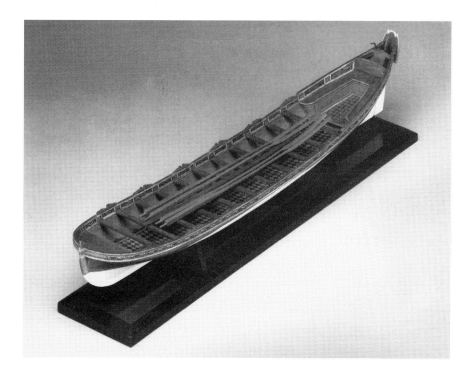

Blanckley's illustration of the twelve-oared barge, with an admiral's flag in the bow. Blanckley's work, published in 1750, probably referred to far older practice, as was common with the publishing of this period when information was disseminated only very slowly. (*E0361*)

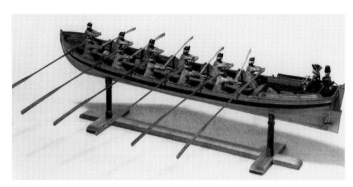

A model of an admiral's barge of around the third quarter of the eighteenth century, complete with figures, the barge crew having a uniform and elaborate headgear. There are eleven of them, but there is a thwart and rowlock for a twelfth. At full size the boat would have been 37ft long with a 7ft beam. (*SLR0332/B9554*)

A draught of a fourteen-oared 32ft barge as built at Portsmouth Dockyard, and dated 6 December 1809. This kind of boat would probably have been issued to 74s and other large two-deckers, especially when carrying an admiral – during the Napoleonic Wars senior officers of detached squadrons often preferred two-deckers rather than cumbersome Second Rates as flagships. (*Bu(d)1*)

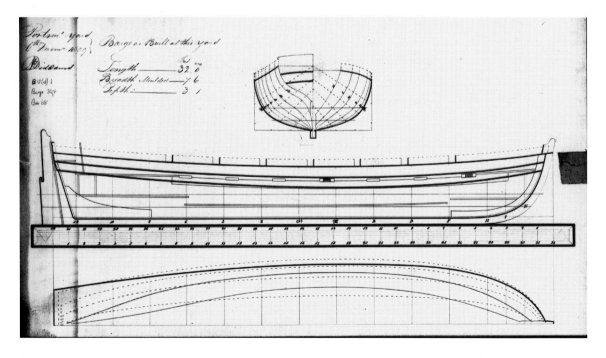

There were state barges, craft designed for the rapid and comfortable conveyance of royalty, government and city dignitaries, and the wealthy, along the waterways provided by rivers. These were often most ornate and to make them light so that they could be rowed swiftly had usually such a low freeboard as to make them quite unsuited to white water. Yet when in 1863 the last two Admiralty barges became redundant someone suggested that they might be adapted for ship use! When it was pointed out that this would be impossible they were sent to Chatham for disposal. There no one had the heart to break them up and they now grace the National Maritime Museum at Greenwich.

It appears that during the war with France, 1689-1697, the Admiral of the Fleet was supplied with a twenty-oared boat in lieu of a pinnace and in 1701 other flag officers desired that they also might have such boats. (In 1716 the Czar successfully coveted the barge of Admiral Sir John Norris.[22]) Approval for this was given and the Master Shipwright at Deptford was directed to build an eighteen-oared boat, 37½ft long, and a sixteen-oared boat, 34½ft long, for a trial to be made to enable a decision to be reached as to the best size of boat for this service.[23] The eighteen-oared boat seems to have been approved for in February 1701/2 we find captains of Third Rates successfully applying for them in lieu of their pinnaces.[24] This was probably the origin of the carrying by some ships of barges instead of pinnaces which was to occur throughout the century. Other flag officers sucessfully solicited the supply of personal boats for their use so that by 1706 the custom of supplying them was firmly established. In that year a twelve-oared boat was ordered for the Third Rate *Torbay* (80), destined to fly the flag of Sir Thomas Dilke, Rear-Admiral of the Red.[25]

Falconer in 1769[26] says that the barge was 'longer slighter and narrower' than a longboat, had never less than ten oars and was used to carry flag officers and captains. In 1815 William Burney's edition of Falconer calls it 'a long, narrow light boat, employed to carry the principal sea-officers, as admirals, and captains of ships of war'. He adds that it is 'very unfit for sea'.[27] It is these two definitions following on that of Blanckley that have led to the general assumption that the barge was essentially the flag officer's personal boat, though in the seventeenth and eighteenth centuries this was not always the case.

It would appear that at one time a barge was allowed in lieu of a pinnace to ships going abroad, for when in 1762 Captain Lord Campbell asked for a barge in lieu of a pinnace for the *Nightingale* (20 guns) he was told by the Navy Board that his ship could not have one unless she was ordered on foreign service.[28] The decision was reversed and a barge was provided shortly after when the *Nightingale* was ordered to the West Indies.

Pinnace is another word whose meaning has altered. Originally they were small seagoing vessels used for scouting and the like, such as the *Anne* and *Discovery* which accompanied Captain John Weddell on his voyage to India and China in 1636-1639. Boteler says:

> As I know no difference between a ship and a pinnace but in the bulk and burthen, so I can take no notice of any difference betwixt a pinnace and a frigate; unless it be in that they have no decks, nor bulkheads, but are all hold below; for otherwise they have the same Masts, yards and shape. And these vessels are much in use with the Spaniards, especially in the West Indies, and so have gotten the denomination of Spanish frigates.[29]

The name pinnace was also given to the large boats which were sometimes taken out in sections for erection when required by ships proceeding on distant expeditions. Three of these were taken by Sir Francis Drake on his expedition to Nombre de Dios in 1572.[30]

As we have seen, the pinnace as a ship's boat had appeared by 1618. It was always rather smaller than the barge and according to Blanckley was intended for the use of the captain.[31] His illustration shows one pulling ten oars

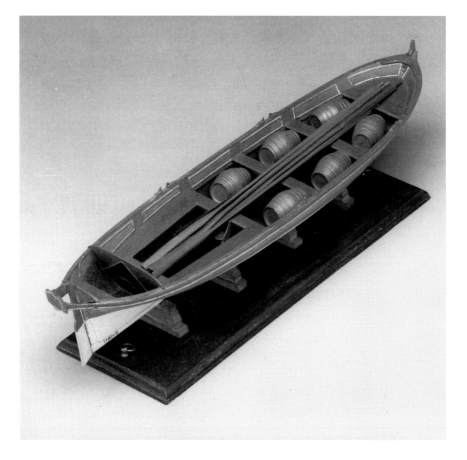

A small pinnace of about 1750 to row with four oars. Although originally catalogued at a scale of ½in to the foot, giving a length of 32ft, it is more likely to be a ¾in scale representing a boat 21ft 6in in length The water butts in this model emphasise one of the chief functions of ships' boats during the age of sail, and even the smallest craft had to be capable of contributing. (SLR0334/D4049D)

Blanckley's pinnace, which resembles his barge, but without the overhanging transom and ten rather than twelve oars. (*E0362*)

A drawing from the sketchbook of the well-known marine artist Nicholas Pocock (1740-1821) reveals how elaborate the decoration of an officer's pinnace might be. Painting the top strakes was not unusual, but the fish symbol on the bow suggests that some boats may have carried heraldic symbols reflecting the name of their ship or commanding officer. (*PAD8876*)

Below A draught of a 28ft pinnace dated September 1793 and re-used with minor alterations for boats ordered in December 1796. This type of boat was allocated to the smaller rates, although in practice many captains preferred cutters by this time. (*Bu(e)1*)

and being of rather broader construction than the barge, but Falconer says: 'Pinnaces exactly resemble barges, only that they are somewhat smaller, and never row more than eight oars; whereas a barge properly never rows less than ten.'[32] Yet in the same year that Falconer's *Dictionary* was published, Captain Walter Stirling of the *Dunkirk* (60 guns) asked that he might have a boat employing fewer men than his ten-oared pinnace.[33]

It would seem from various references that barges and pinnaces were often carried rather indiscriminately by ships and used for the majority of work for which a large boat was required, but the weighty longboat was unnecessary. With boats so similar there was evidently some confusion as to the difference between a barge and a pinnace and this is shown in 1722. The *Salisbury* (54 guns) and *Exeter* (60), two Fourth Rates, lent their barges with

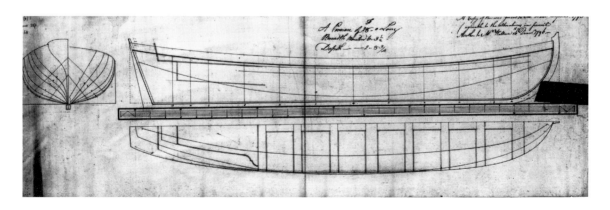

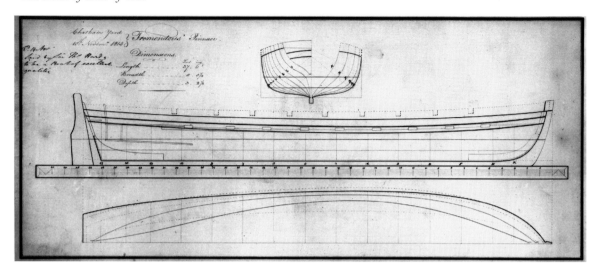

a party of men to help the East India Company at Bombay in a small expedition against the Portuguese.[34] In the report of the East India Company's representatives the boats are described as pinnaces.[35] It is noteworthy that on this voyage of 1721-1724 these two private ships carried barges, while the *Lyon* (64), another Fourth Rate wearing the broad pendant of Commodore Thomas Mathews, had a barge and a pinnace in addition. The pinnace fell to pieces while it was being hoisted out in the Hooghly.[36]

In the eighteenth century there was a tendency for the Admiralty to call boats by the number of their oars rather than by the type. It is quite likely that a boat which had been issued to one ship as a pinnace might subsequently be issued by the dockyard to a smaller ship as a barge. When a boat was issued to a ship for service as the barge of a flag officer it was fitted with an awning, curtains and cushions, usually of green damask, and 'freezed'. An instance of this occurred in 1771 when Rear-Admiral Lord Howe chose a ten-oared boat instead of a twelve to serve as a barge for him in the *Barfleur* (98) and it was subsequently fitted accordingly.[37]

The barge and pinnace replaced the cokkeboat of earlier times, which had hardly survived into the seventeenth century, though it is mentioned by Boteler about 1634 as having become much smaller that it had been originally. He says, 'There are usually no other Boats but those that are to be hoisted in; for as for those Cock-boats, Wherries, and the like, they are but seldom used, and are indeed too tender and small to do any Service at Sea.'[38]

The **shallop** was rather smaller than the pinnace and references to it are few. Those by John Smith[39] in 1627, and Nathaniel Boteler[40] in 1634, besides Sir Henry Mainwaring[41] in 1644 suggest that it was an alternative name for a skiff. Apart from the *Prince/Prince Royal* in 1618 and 1627 the only other ship I have found carrying one was the *Monmouth* (66 guns) under Sir Thomas Allin in 1668.[42]

A draught of a 37ft 6in eighteen-oared pinnace, 'said by Sir Thomas Hardy to be a boat of excellent qualities'; the pinnace was from the 74-gun *Tremendous*. Dated 10 November 1815, this boat was probably proposed to Admiral Byam Martin's committee looking into the revision and standardisation of stores and equipment for the post-war navy. *(Bu(e)24)*

There is in the National Maritime Museum a boat which has always been known as the Queen's Shallop. It was built for Queen Mary in 1689, is 41ft 6in long and 6ft 6in beam, pulling ten oars, single-banked. The robust nature of her construction is such that she was probably built on the lines of a ship's shallop, but larger.

Another boat occasionally encountered was the **wherry**, light and fast. An indirect tribute to its speed will be found in the logbook of the *Hunter* (30) for 13 December 1679. Her first lieutenant had said of a pirate vessel that he could not get near her for 'shee sailed like a fish, and rowed like a Wherrie'.[43] The wherry first appears in the fifteenth century.[44] In 1595, during Sir Walter Raleigh's voyage the *Lions's Whelp* had a 'bote' and 'wherrie'.[45] Boteler about 1634 classes the wherry with the 'Cock-Bote' as 'beinge too tender and small to perform any service when a shipp is abroad att sea'.[46]

A contemporary model of a shallop thought to have been built in 1691 for King William III, which explains the high level of decoration. It is therefore not a ship's boat, but the ship-borne version of the shallop probably shared the same fine-lined hull form optimised for rowing – in this case, eight oars, single-banked with the option of two extra in the bow and stern. (*SLR0380/D4986*)

In 1660-1661 the *Plymouth* (60) caried a wherry in addition to a long-boat and pinnace,[47] but this boat dropped out of use completely in favour of the jollyboat, as the jollywatt came to be called, for I have been unable to find any other case of one being carried by a man-of-war. It is true that Blanckley[48] mentions the wherry amonst other boats, but by this time it had become, for the Navy at any rate, a dockyard boat only.

The journals of Sir Thomas Allin, 1660-1670,[49] throw some light on boats carried at the period. From them it would appear that the *Plymouth*, in 1660-1661 had a longboat, launch, pinnace and wherry. It seems possible that the launch may have been a replacement for a lost longboat. In

1664-1665 the same ship carried a longboat, pinnace and jollyboat. It will be observed that the jollywatt of some forty years earlier has modernised its name, but it was soon to drop out of the Navy for about a century.

Blanckley's yawl, a six-oared boat. (*E0363*)

It was at this period that a new type of small boat called a **yawl** came into the Royal Navy and soon squeezed out the jollyboat, though the two for a time remained in service side by side. Sir Thomas Allin's first mention of a yawl was on 1 May 1662 when one was given to him by the Chevalier Francisco Panetie.[50] Allin's early spelling 'yoll' and 'youll' suggest a Scandinavian origin and indeed these boats were sometimes referred to as 'Norway yawls'. Later they were generally built at Deal so were called 'Deal Yawls'. These were clinker-built boats. The true Norway yawls had pointed sterns, but this feature was lacking from the Deal yawls.

Sir Thomas Allin was in the Mediterranean again in 1668–1669, this time in the *Monmouth* (66 guns). He says that she had five boats, a longboat, barge, shallop, jollyboat and yawl. It is of course possible that he is using the two latter names for the same boat. Lest it be thought that the barge was an additional boat, carried by Allin as a flag officer, it must be mentioned that he

Below A draught showing the boats of the sloop *Swift*, a name unfortunately too common to be certain of the date, but probably the 1741 vessel. The boat at the top is 21ft by 5ft 9½ in and clinker-built and may be an early yawl; the curved sternpost is unusual. The lower vessel, drawn at a smaller scale, is actually longer at about 24ft and is probably a pinnace. (*Bu(h)2*)

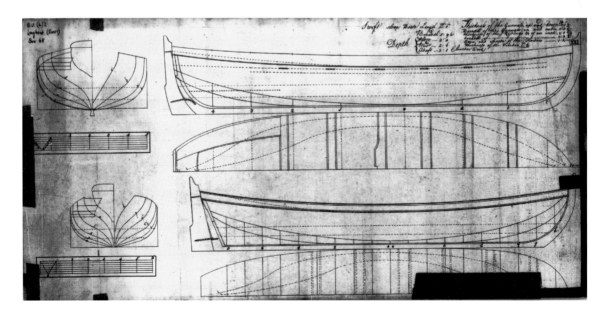

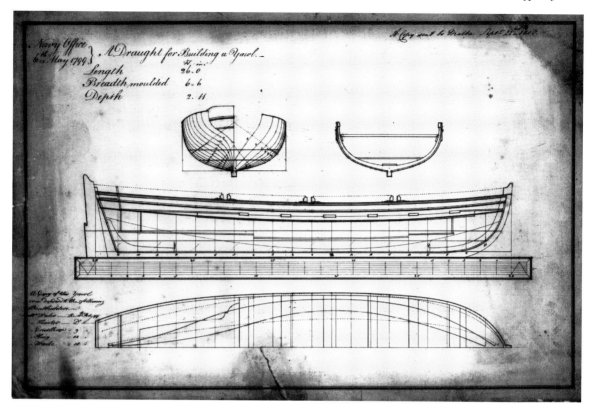

A draught of a 26ft yawl, dated 6 May 1799. Annotations reveal that copies were sent to five different boatbuilders the previous February so was obviously built in numbers; a copy was also sent to Malta nearly a decade later, in September 1808, so it must have been a satisfactory design. Note the (removable?) wash-strake indicated in ticked line. (*Bu(c)17*)

prefixes the names of the boats with a number of conflicting pronouns – 'our longboat', 'my longboat', 'the barge', 'our barge', 'my barge', 'the jollyboat', 'my jollyboat', 'my yawl', 'our yawl', 'the yawl'.

On 15 June 1669 the Duke of York thought it necessary when giving instructions for the conduct of the Mediterranean fleet to say that: 'as the said Fleet may in all probability have occasion for an extraordinary number of Boates in the service they are going upon; I desire that you will take care for furnishing each shipp of the Third Rate and also ye St David with three Boates.' The *St David* was a Fourth Rate of 54 guns.

About 1672 we have an establishment of the number of boats allowed to different types of ships, though it is likely that this had been in force for some time previously. It unfortunately does not give the lengths of the boats. From this establishment it appears that only First Rates and Second Rates of 70 guns and over carried three boats apiece. Two boats were allowed to Second Rates of less than 70 guns, to Third, Fourth and Fifth Rates and to the Sixth Rates *Golden Hand, Friesland, Hardrene* and *Francis*, fireship. All other Sixth Rates carried a single boat only.[51]

Another inventory of 1685[52] mentions a longboat for each of the first five rates and a pinnace for all six. Apparently the existence of the smallest boat was overlooked. That it still existed is clear from another inventory, that

of the *Duchess* of 1679, who was supplied with a 32ft longboat, a 31ft pinnace and a 20ft skiff. The apparent interchange of the name skiff for what was evidently a jollyboat or yawl will be noted.

In time of war there is always a tendency for a bending of the regulations, to be followed at its conclusion by a tightening up. In 1698 the Navy Board noticed that the yards, instead of supplying boats from store which were quite suitable, had been building special boats to meet the desires of officers. This practice was ordered to cease.[53]

In 1701 the establishment for each Fourth Rate was increased to three boats by the addition of a Deal Yawl 'to prevent damage that often happens to their pinnaces when employed on such services which such yawls are more proper for'. The 60-gun ships were to have six-oared and the 50-gun ships four-oared boats.[54]

In the following year an eight-oared yawl was added to the establishments of First, Second and Third Rates, increasing their allowance of boats to four or three as the case might be. These boats were to be built in the yards 'after the manner of a Deal Yawl in all respects, except in the clinker work'.[55] The implication that previous yawls built at Deal had been clinker-built will be noted. From this and other evidence it is clear that clinker-built boats were a speciality of the Deal boatbuilders.

Complaints concerning the boats supplied were by no means unusual. In April 1709 Captain James Gunman of the *Lyme* (32 guns) wrote to the Admiralty to suggest that his ship might be allowed a yawl instead of her longboat:

> which Longboat cannot be hoisted in without disableing the Guns on the Deck where the main force of the ship lies and unshipping the Jeer Capstern, which are both very great inconveniencys neither can she be hoisted upp and hang'd over the Side without very apparent danger of my Masts itt being altogether unsafe, and should I either chace or be chaced I shall be obliged to cutt her away she being a great hindrance to the Ships way. And a Yawle of twenty one foot long will be subject to none of these inconveniencys and will be sufficient to water the ship or to carry out a Stream anchor to heave the ship of should she happen to touch the ground, in any weather that my longboat can carry out a bower anchor in.[56]

In a second letter written a few days later he said of the longboat, 'neither can she be lash't to the gunhill with safety or carryed any other ways then being towed at the Stern.'[57]

Apparently Captain Gunman got his yawl, but very shortly after it was smashed by a collier. The *Lyme* was issued by the Navy Board with a new longboat and in October Captain Gunman had to beg for a yawl all over again.[58] The Navy Board were very averse to the change. They said that it was common for officers to make similar applications to them,[59] but it had always been the establishment that every ship, whatever her size, should have a longboat and 'wee have not Judged it proper for us to dispence there-with,' because 'some ships and Companys having been Lost, and several other inconveniencys attending the Service from the want thereof'.[60]

In 1710 the Admiralty returned to the question of the suitability of the longboats in use. The difficulty attending hoisting them in the lower rates and the inconvenience of towing them often led officers to leave their long-boats behind when going to sea and when frigates lay in the Downs in winter their boats were often incapable of handling their anchors and cables or of fetching such things from the shore so that Deal hookers had to be hired to do the work.[61] It is probable that as a result of these searchings the sizes of longboats were reduced, for in general they became shorter than the barges and pinnaces. Hoisting in boats of suitable size by the smallest vessels always however remained a difficulty and as late as 1780 we find the cutter *Advice*, Lieutenant Swann, losing her boat which she was towing because it was too big to hoist.[62]

During the first quarter of the eighteenth century a new type of boat appears on the scene, though it was some time before it came into anything like general use. This was the **cutter**, clinker-built like other boats that had originated at Deal and described thus by Falconer in 1769:

> broader, deeper, and shorter than barges and pinnaces, they are fitter for sail-ing, and are commonly employed in carrying stores, provisions, passengers, &c. to and from the ship. In the structure of this sort of boat, the lower-edge of every plank in the side over-lays the upper-edge of the plank below, which is called by shipwrights clinch-work.[63]

Draught of a 28ft cutter 'taken off at Woolwich 1764'. She appears to pull eight oars, single-banked, and had a permanent wash-strake. Note the mast clamp on the thwart admidships and the ring bolts on the keelson for hoisting (*Bu(b)10*)

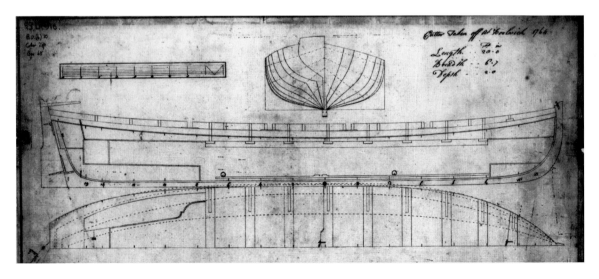

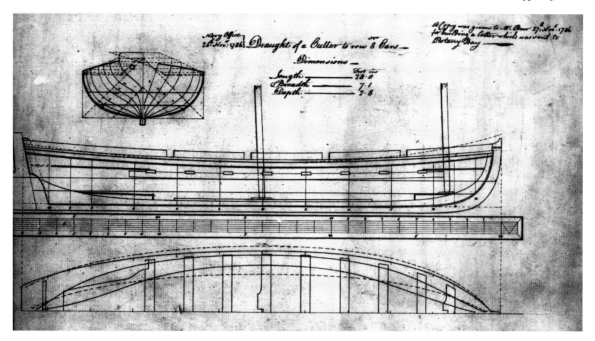

A later version of an eight-oared 28ft cutter, 24 November 1786. Slightly broader at 7ft 1in compared with the 6ft 7in of the 1764 draught, this boat is also rather flatter in the floors. The draught, which unusually shows the masts stepped, is annotated: 'A copy was given to Mr Burr 27 November 1786 for building a cutter which was sent to Botany Bay'. (*Bu(b)1*)

Cutters could be single- or double-banked. Falconer illustrated a 28ft cutter of 8½ft beam, pulling ten oars double-banked. He clearly shows what has always been a feature of cutters, that the oars will work in rowlocks cut in the top strake. This enables the boat to be built with a higher freeboard while the men can still row with their oars at a convenient height above their thwarts. This feature contrasts with other boats of the period in which the oars were always constrained between thole pins above the top strake.

The earliest mention that I have been able to find concerning a cutter is in the Deal Letter Books of 1712.[64] In the summer of that year the *Rochester* (54), Captain Aldred, was at Kinsale, where she lost her pinnace. The captain does not appear to have bothered about the loss until July, when at his request the Navy Board instructed Deal to issue him with a new one. The Navy Board should have known that Deal did not stock spare boats of this type and the Naval Officer there replied that, as the *Rochester* had two yawls of six and five oars respectively and always left her pinnace behind when cruising, she could quite well manage without a replacement until she reached one of the yards and could get a pinnace. This did not suit Captain Aldred and for eight pounds he bought what he called 'a Deal Yaule of Twenty foot long'[65] and what the Naval Officer described as 'a Second hand small Cutter about 20ft long which could not be of any service to the Ship and which sort of Boats you have lately forbid the building or buying for her Majts Shipps'.

In May 1720 the Naval Officer at Deal described an eighteen-oared yawl which had been specially built for the *Dursley Galley* as 'between a Cutter

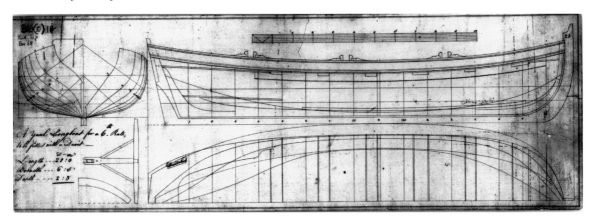

and a sailing boat'.[66] In the following year the *Lyon* (64) took a cutter with her to India, for it is recorded in her log-book under the date of 3 April 1722 that the longboat and cutter were sent away to get turtle at Mauritius.[67]

In April 1740 the Admiralty approved a plan originated by the Navy Board for supplying each ship of the First, Second and Third rates with an additional boat to aid them in pressing men. These were to be 25ft six-oared boats or Deal Cutters.[68] During that summer cutters were ordered to be built at Deal for various services,[69] culminating in the provision of four for the *Centurion* (50), *Gloucester* (50), *Severn* (48) and *Wager* (24), shortly to depart with Commodore George Anson on his expedition to the South Seas. There must have been some purchases of cutters for the Navy in the previous years for when the first three were supplied to his ships from Portsmouth Anson complained that they were 'very old and unfit for the Service of the Voyage'.[70] The *Centurion*'s cutter was a 22ft boat and with that of the *Gloucester* was left to cruise off Acapulco in the spring of 1742 to watch for the Manila galleon. Later in the same year the *Centurion*'s cutter with a lieutenant and six men cruised independently off the same port for forty-three days, rejoining on the 5 May.[71]

The lengths of cutters in use in about 1767 varied between 15ft and 28ft, but the Navy could not be content even with this spread of dimensions and had to produce a hybrid called a cutter-yawl.[72] Perhaps, however, I have mis-understood this statement and that what the writer intended was a some-what careless abbreviation for a cutter-built yawl. When yawls had first been taken into the service they were generally built at Deal, where the boat-builders concentrated their efforts on clinker-built boats, so that all yawls were clinker-built. Then the building of yawls was largely transferred to the naval dockyards, where all boats were carvel-built. Deal next developed the cutter, again a clinker-built boat and, as the clinker-built yawls became scarcer, this type of construction became associated almost exclusively with the cutter and hence a clinker-built boat of any other type came to be known colloquially as cutter-built.

'A yawl longboat for a 6th Rate, to be fitted with a davit.' Although undated, this draught of a 21ft boat relates to the kind of craft supplied in lieu of a conventional long-boat to small frigates and sloops from the middle of the eighteenth century. The davit with its sheave, used for handling anchor cables, is drawn separately. *(Bu(c)18)*

'Getting up a kedge anchor', an engraving by J A Atkinson published in 1807 showing the use of the stern davit in a boat about the size of the yawl longboat shown above. (*PAD7764*)

It is one of the irritations which accompany historical research that one so often finds that some particular source of information which might have been expected to be easily available and to provide the information required has nevertheless disappeared completely. An example is the total lack of the establishment of stores for the various rates of ships. These definitely existed but none can now be traced with the exception of one or two from the seventeenth century which have already been discussed. It is true that corrections to these establishments which were made at various times can be found, but they leave much to be desired, being widely spaced out and very incomplete. There was evidently a gradual increase in the numbers of boats allowed to ships. Some of these additions were promulgated from time to time and these we will now consider.

In 1715, on the recommendation of the Navy Board, approval was given for 20 and 24-gun ships to carry two boats instead of one – a 27ft pinnace and a 17ft Deal Yawl, the latter having 'a Trunck fixed in the Midships, and a Windless so fitted as to weigh and carry out an Anchor'.[73] This fitting of a 'Trunck' instead of a davit is here mentioned for the first time as far as I am aware. It antedates by about a century the proposals of John Cow.[74]

In 1740 a cutter was added to the establishment of ships of the first three rates, increasing their allowance to five and four boats.[75] The issue of a

Blanckley's illustrations of a longboat and a launch. To emphasise the more ship-like qualities of the former, she is shown under sail, but the flatter and broader launch is seen under oars. *(E0361&E0364)*

cutter was quickly extended to Fourth Rates also for these boats were carried by the ships of Anson's squadron in 1740.[76] In 1769 the Fourth Rate *Dunkirk* (60), preparing to sail with the Commander-in-Chief for Jamaica, had a longboat, a 10-oared pinnace, a cutter and a yawl, besides a barge for Commodore Arther Forrest. Her captain was allowed to exchange her pinnace and yawl for two more cutters and her longboat for one of the larger type carried by a 74-gun ship. This would probably have been 31ft long.[77]

In 1761 a new scale of boats for the smaller vessels was introduced.[78] Frigates of 36 and 32 guns had a 23ft longboat, a 30ft pinnace and a 24ft yawl, while those of 28 and 24 guns carried a 22ft or 21ft longboat, a 28ft pinnace and a 23ft or 22ft yawl. We see here how the frigate's longboat has shrunk in size until it is now shorter even than the yawl. Sloops had 16–19ft longboats and 24–26ft pinnaces. They were not allowed yawls, but in 1777 the larger sloops of 16 guns and 300 or more tons were granted an 18ft, four-oared cutter in addition.[79]

During the Seven Years War (1756–1763) it became customary for frigates and sloops to depart from the establishment and for their captains to obtain those boats which they thought most suitable for their cruising stations and to rely when in harbour on the loan of boats from local sources or from ships of the line. The cutter became extremely popular. 'In War time they are very useful to cruizing Ships; for altho' they are generally the worst rowing Boats, yet they will live longest in a great Sea, and are very proper for boarding Ships in bad weather and shifting Prisoners.' On the other hand 'Cutters, of all Boats are the slightest, the most subject to be out of order and the most difficult to repair: they are unfit for carrying Anchors, Cables, Water cask &c. therefore but badly supply the place of Longboats'.[80]

Lord Colvill, the Commander-in-Chief in North America, wrote to the

Right A fine little contemporary model of the longboat for the *Medway*, a 60-gun Fourth Rate of 1749. If the scale is accurate, the full-size length would be 28ft, and the boat rows sixteen oars double-banked. The windlass amidships is a prominent feature. *(SLR0329/D4057)*

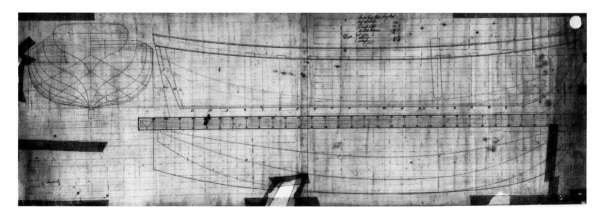

A draught for an 80-gun ship's 33ft longboat. The style of the draught, and the proportions of the boat, suggest a date of about 1740. *(Bu(h)12)*

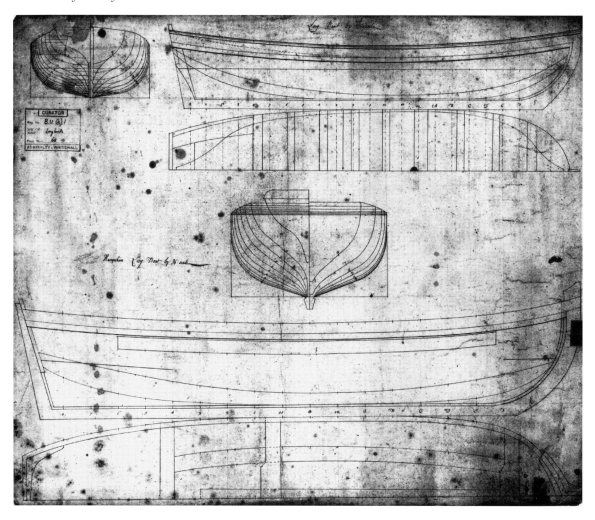

Admiralty in 1764 of the diversity of boats carried by the ships under his command. Of the 28-gun frigates the *Maidstone* had a longboat-yawl, a 10-oared barge and a six-oared yawl; the *Mermaid* had a ten-oared barge and two cutters, one of which was replaced locally by a four-oared yawl when it was washed overboard, and the *Coventry* also had a barge and two cutters. Of the three 20-gun frigates two, the *Guarland* and *Squirrel*, had each a long-boat-yawl and a cutter while the *Alborough* had an eight-oared pinnace and a cutter. Each of the two 14-gun sloops had a four-oared cutter, the *Fortune* having in addition a six-oared cutter, the *Senegal* an eight-oared boat of unspecified type. The longboat-yawls were of varying dimensions and were not always designed for the work they had to do. All were 'heavy Rowers'. This diversity suggest that they were not built to Navy Board specifications but tht they were odd boats obtained from various sources in the exigencies of wartime.

Colvill proposed a new establishment of boats for frigates and sloops. In

Another early longboat draught, marked 'Hampshirs', presumably a reference to the 50-gun *Hampshire* of 1741; it shows an unusually sharp section. The more conventional form of the boat above must be of contemporary date, but is drawn at ½in to the foot compared with ¾in for the lower draught. *(Bu(h)1)*

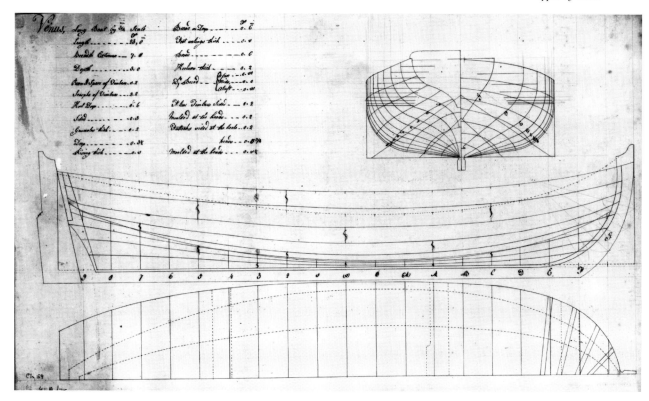

A 23ft longboat for the 36-gun frigate *Venus* of 1758. This draught also lists the principal scantlings, and indicates the shift of butts in the carvel strakes. This was the size that became established for the larger frigates in 1769. (*Ch59*)

A late example of a longboat, 'built by the desire of Admiral Keppel, August 1778'. It measured 27ft by 9ft 2in and is unusually broad and deep. (*Bu(h)3*)

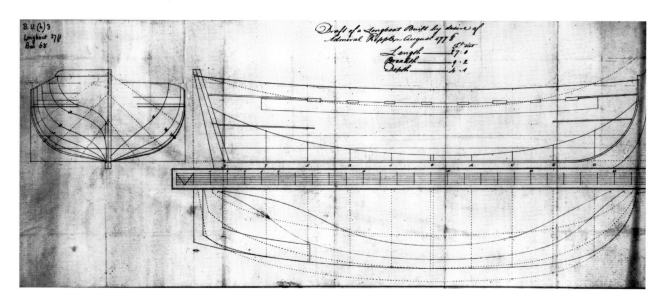

his opinion every frigate should have a 28ft pinnace which is of 'sufficient Breadth and not too fine a Bottom ... will answer most Ends better than a Barge, and . . . would be preferred by the generality of Captains of Ships under the Line of Battle'. Every frigate should have a longboat, those for 28- and 32-gun frigates being 24ft long and 8ft beam. One of these would carry two tons of water in butts or puncheons or three tons in hogsheads. They should be 'full abaft for weighing or carrying out Anchors, and flatt like a launch for stowing under the Booms'. For 20-gun frigates the longboat might have to be rather smaller. As a third boat all frigates should carry 'a neat four-oared yawl to be built after the manner of the Pinnace'.

Sloops of 14 guns and upwards should carry a 19ft longboat of 6ft 4in beam, which would carry six hogsheads, and a six-oared yawl built like a pinnace. Finally every frigate and sloop should carry in addition a cutter, if she could conveniently stow it.

The reference in Colvill's report to the carrying of barges by the *Maidstone* and *Mermaid* although they were private ships provides one more proof, if it were needed, that at this time barges were not the sole prerogative of flag officers.

A new establishment of boats for frigates and sloops was introduced in 1769. Lord Colvill's recommendation that they should carry cutters was ignored. The approved lengths of boats for the various ships were as follows:

	Frigates of guns				*Sloops of guns*		
	36	32	28	24	16	14	10
Longboat	23ft	23ft	22ft	21ft	19ft	18ft	16ft
Pinnace	30ft	30ft	28ft	28ft	26ft	25ft	24ft
Yawl	24ft	24ft	23ft	22ft			

When one of these ships was ordered for Channel service the yawl was to be clinker-built, like a cutter. For foreign service it was to be carvel-built.[81]

It must have been about this time that the ships of the line increased the number of boats that they carried. A table of boat spars laid down in 1771[82] would appear to indicate that a 74-gun ship now carried six, namely a longboat, a barge, a pinnace, a yawl and two cutters of different lengths. In 1781 the boats ordered to be built locally for the *Excellent* (74), which was on the slip at Harwich, consisted of a 31ft launch, 32ft and 28ft pinnaces, and three cutters, two of 25ft and one of 18ft.[83] The 18ft cutter had recently been added to the establishment of all ships down to 20 guns.[84]

A small 18ft cutter, undated but about 1800, of the kind that came to be called a jollyboat. *(Bu(b)5)*

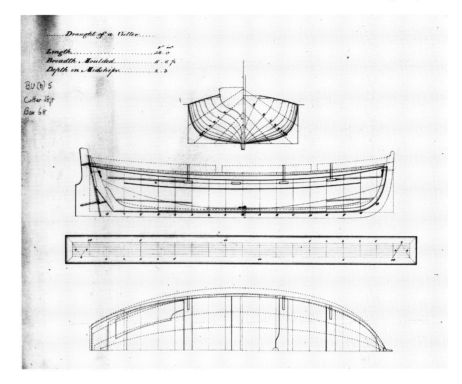

The ordering of a launch instead of a longboat for the *Excellent* will have been noted. The **launch** was originally a dockyard boat. It was described by Blanckley in 1750 as being 'Made use of by the Masters Attendant for transporting Ships, are built of great Breadth, and low to the Water for the more conveniently coyling transporting Hawsers in'.[85] J J Moore in 1801 compares it with the longboat as being 'longer, more flat-bottomed, and by rowing a greater number of oars, is better adapted for going up narrow and shallow rivers'.[86]

The launch was occasionally used as a ship's boat. One is mentioned as belonging to the *Plymouth* by Sir Thomas Allin on 2 and 27 August 1661,[87] in addition to her longboat, pinnace and wherry. On 25 March 1740, Captain Richard Norris of the *Gloucester* (50) asked for a launch instead of a longboat before sailing with Anson for the South Seas.[88] It was refused, but on 27 July 1742 Captain Edward Boscawen stated that he had 'experienced the use and convenience of a Launch preferable to a Longboat, in the expeditious watering, carrying of Stores, and towing of the Ship, as well as the Carrying a great Number of hands on any occasion, with much greater conveniency for Stowage on Deck'.[89]

The Admiralty sought the advice of the Navy Board on this matter and it in turn consulted the dockyards. The Deptford Officers replied that they had no personal experience, but they had heard that the East Indiaman *Prince Frederick* had tried a 37ft 5in launch of sixteen oars instead of a longboat and had found it very satisfactory. They suggested building a launch 36ft long and 10ft beam for the *Dreadnought* to try.[90] This was approved.[91]

Two other similar requests followed very rapidly; from Captain Charles Dennison of the *Orford* (70)[92] and from Captain Franklin Lushington of the *Burford* (70).[93] The former of these was approved, it being thought that the experiment was better tried by two ships than by one. The *Burford* was at first refused, but within a fortnight the Board had changed its mind. The *Burford* and *Suffolk* (70), Captain Charles Knowles, were under orders for the West Indies and it was thought that launches, carrying more men, might be more suitable than longboats for the combined operations that were envisaged. Orders were accordingly given that these two ships were to be given the launches ordered for the *Orford* and *Dreadnought*, two new launches being built for the last-named ships. Each of the two launches for the *Burford* and *Suffolk* was to be fitted with stocks for mounting six swivel guns.[94]

While undoubtedly the greater beaminess of the launch over the longboat enabled more water to be carred per trip, one would have thought her less seaworthy and less capable of carrying sail, so that the longboat would

'A draught for building a launch by Mr Burr at Rotherhithe to row 14 oars double banked', dated Navy Office 22 March 1779. A 29ft boat, the windlass and davit are noticeable features. (*Bu(a)37*)

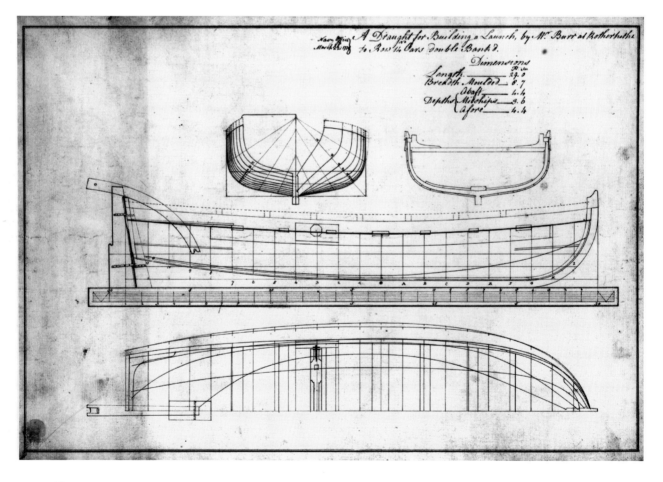

have been the better compromise. Nevertheless, requests for launches in lieu of longboats continued to be made occasionally (for example for the *Montagu* (60) in the Mediterranean in 1757 and for the *Superb* (74) in the Channel in 1762, both commanded by Captain Sir Joshua Rowley,[95] and the *Barfleur* (98), Captain Andrew Snape Hamond in 1771[96]) and finally on 7 November 1780 orders were originated for supplying all ships down to those of 20 guns, which were building or repairing, with launches instead of longboats and so longboats gradually dropped out of use.[97]

Although the jollyboat had disappeared from the Royal Navy before the end of the seventeenth century, it is evident that this name for a small boat continued in occasional use in the English language and it is probable that it was never entirely dropped. In 1742 the boatbuilder of Deptford Dockyard was ordered to build a yawl for the *Liverpool* (28), and provided her instead with a Sixth Rate's longboat. Asked to explain his action he replied to the Navy Board that 'a yawl of twenty one Feet long was Demanded & Ordered by your Warrant of the 29th October last and no otherwise distinguished either as a Jollyboat or Pinnace built of that length as is sometimes

One of the chief design requirements of a launch was its ability to carry water casks. This 33ft launch for a Second Rate could stow fourteen of the largest 'leaguers', each of which contained 150 gallons. This design was approved by the Admiralty on 12 May 1804. (*Bu(a)79*)

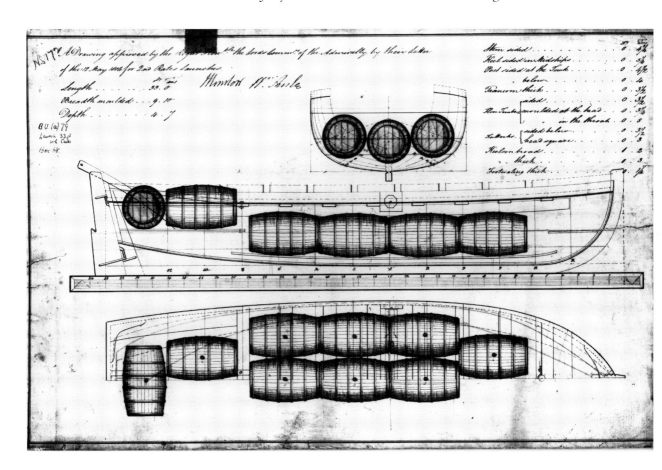

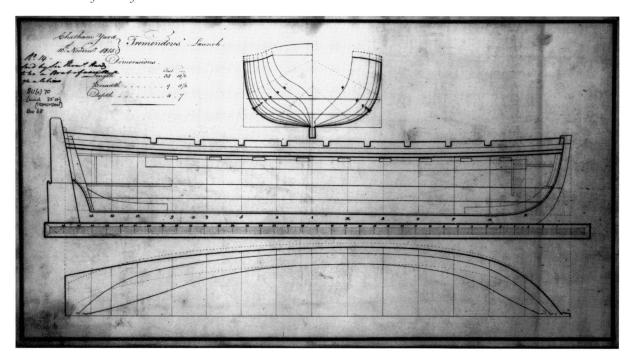

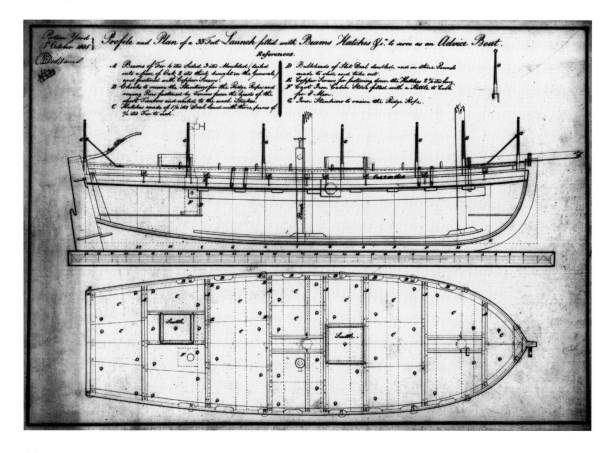

customary'[98]. The use of the name Jollyboat is very interesting, but the excuse seems an inadequate explanation for why a longboat was built instead of a yawl.

In the latter years of the eighteenth century the small 16ft or 18ft four-oared cutter became known as the jollyboat.[99] After a while it became known officially as a cutter or jolly boat, indiscriminately, the first such use which I have been able to find of the latter name being in 1795.[100] From a predilection for using the jollyboat for bringing off fresh meat it was, during the first half of the nineteenth century, known colloquially as the 'blood boat'.[101]

The word 'gigge' or 'giggish' as an adjective meaning light or flighty has been traced back to 1225, but kindred usage as a noun is not generally thought to have come into use before 1780, when it was used for a flighty girl, in 1790 for a type or boat and in 1791 for a light carriage.[102]

Below Ship's boats in action: the frigate *Thetis* aground off the North Carolina coast, 23 December 1794. Having carried out anchors to kedge the ship off, the two boats in the foreground are sounding with lead-line to find deep water. A third boat hooks on at the stern – later illustrations in this water-colour sequence show the frigate to have stern davits, even at this early date, and since they were done on the spot by George Tobin, one of her lieutenants, it is safe to assume they are right. The ship was hauled off safely with the aid of the frigate *Cleopatra*, and repaired at Gosport, Virginia. (*PAG9750*)

Above left A draught of a launch, 'said by Sir Thomas Hardy to be a boat of excellent qualities'; like the pinnace reproduced earlier it was from the 74-gun *Tremendous*. Dated 10 November 1815, this boat was 35ft 10½in long and rowed eighteen oars. (*Bu(a)70*)

Left Launches were large enough to operate almost entirely independently from their mother ship, and in areas like the Caribbean often functioned as tenders cruising against small privateers and coastal traders. However, this draught demonstrates how a makeshift conversion can turn a 33ft launch into a decked advice boat for the carriage of orders and intelligence. The deck is made up of a series of hatches, with a tiny cuddy aft that contained a cast iron cabin stove fitted with a 'kettle' to cook for the crew of eight men. Weather-cloths lashed to a series of iron stanchions would have given some slight protection to the decks, and the boat has a two-masted rig with a bowsprit and probably set lug sails. (*Bu(a)91*)

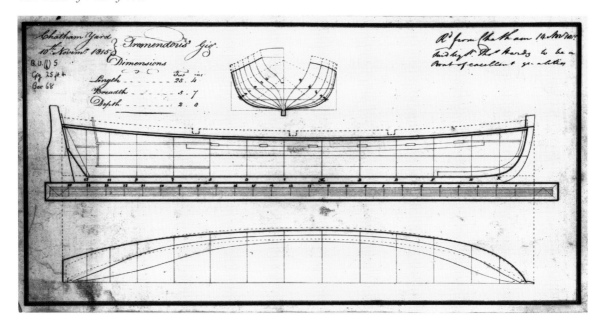

When the Seven Years War came to an end in 1763, the Admiralty purchased thirty cutters and in that and the following year built six more. These cutters must not be confused with the cutters which were ships' boats. They were small seagoing vessels measuring about 40-60ft on the gundeck, and the Admiralty intended to station them around the coasts to cruise against smugglers. It was thought that the boats which were carried by the purchased vessels were often unsuitable for the naval service and Deal was instructed to build twelve cutters for them. Mr Benjamin, the Naval Officer there, sought the advice of four boatbuilders of that town and informed the Navy Board that 'they are confident that the 25 & 24 feet Cutters in these Stores are not what is wanted to answer the Purpose of suppressing the Smugglers. But a sort of Boats vulgarly called giggs of 21 feet long that are much used on this Coast, being excessive light and handy will bear almost any wear'. He went on to recommend that **gigs** should be built for the cutters 24ft long, 6ft 4in broad and 2ft 2in deep with a light fixed washstrake 5in high, and carrying two sails, a lug foresail and a mizen.[103]

The Navy Board approved this proposal and told Benjamin to have gigs built instead of cutters for the purchased vessels. Thus the gig came into the Royal Navy. (In subsequent correspondence Benjamin called these boats 'giggs' or 'cutter giggs' indescriminately.) The beam proposed for these early boats seems to be rather excessive. A drawing given by Burney in 1815 shows a 25ft gig with a beam of only 5ft.[104]

During the French Wars captains began to find the use of a small boat, which could be quickly got in and out, more convenient than the clumsy barge. Many of them therefore took to acquiring and carrying to sea small

With the gradual replacement of pinnaces and barges by cutters, senior officers came to desire fast-rowing boats for their personal transport and gigs were the popular response. This 25ft 4in gig is another of Hardy's recommended boats from the *Tremendous* and again said by him to possess excellent qualities. (*Bu(f)5*)

light boats which were their own property and there were many occasions that orders were given that these boats were not to be repaired or painted by the use of ship's stores. In 1794 a few captains were allowed to exchange their pinnaces for eight-oared cutters. They then appropriated these cutters for their own personal use, while keeping the barges allowed to them on the booms. Thus the other officers were deprived of the use of a boat. Orders were given that no more pinnaces might be exchanged for cutters but that barges might be exchanged for them.[105] This illustrates the desire of captains for a smaller and more convenient boat than the heavy ones which had previously been considered necessary to support their dignity.

The favourite of private boats became the long light single-banked gig, originally brought into the Navy for the use of small vessels. The earliest reference to this which I have found was one used by Nelson when he was in the Baltic in the *Elephant* in 1801.[106] The first official mention of gigs in vessels other than cutters dates from 1808 when the establishment of brig-sloops of 235 tons was altered from two gigs and a jolly boat to a 24ft cutter, a gig and a 14ft jollyboat to facilitate watering. The displaced gig was 25ft in length. This alteration to an establishment shows that gigs were already allowed to vessels other than cutters.

Captain Marryat makes several references to gigs in his novel *Frank Mildmay*. Although this is fiction the book is based on the author's actual experience during the latter part of the French Wars, and it therefore throws light upon actual conditions. The hero is made to take part in the fireship attack on Basque Roads on 11 April 1809, where it is said: 'we had a four-oared gig, a small narrow thing (misnamed by the sailors a 'coffin'), to make our escape in'.[107] One of Mildmay's captains had a private gig actually built on board by the carpenter using government timber, the main planks cut from a spare anchor stock.[108] There is a vivid picture of a smart frigate's gig: 'The frigate hove to; soon after the gig was lowered down, and came to fetch me; a clean cloak was spread in the stern sheets; the men were dressed in white frocks and trowsers, as clean as hands could make them, with neat straw hats, and canvas shoes'.[109]

HOISTING BOATS

Boats had always been hoisted in by means of tackles attached to the fore and main yardarms. It was a cumbersome business and it is surprising that it lasted so long.

In the 1790s an additional system was introduced. Davits were for the first time fitted on each quarter of ships for hoisting two of the lighter boats, usually cutters. At sea these boats could be griped against the davits and

Stages in the development of boat stowage.

1. The waist of the frigate *Lowestoffe* of 1761 still shows the pinnace stowed on a pair of spare topmasts. At this date the 32-gun ship was also established with a 23ft longboat and a 24ft yawl, so it is hardly surprising that many captains cruising in home waters often left at least one of their heavier boats on shore. (*SLR0339/C231*)

2. This unidentified frigate model of about 1800 includes a launch and two cutters (although it should have a further two boats); these are stowed on removable transverse beams between the narrow gangways, along with the spare spars. The model has no quarter davits. (*SLR0346/D4080-E*)

3. The next step was to widen the gangways and make them flush with the forecastle and quarterdeck, supported by fixed beams across the waist to take the weight of more boats. This slightly crude model, which purports to represent the *Pomone*, 38 of 1805, is one of the few to include more boats than the proper establishment, but is interesting in showing the fixed stern davits introduced in the 1790s. These were used to handle a sea-boat, most commonly the smallest cutter called the jollyboat. One of the boats is suspended from the stay tackles, which, together with the yard tackles, was the cumbersome method of getting the boats into the water before the advent of davits. (*SLR0651/A962*)

boats so hoisted could be lifted more easily and more quickly than by the old method. Boats hoisted at davits came often to be called quarter-boats. According to Admiral of the Fleet Sir Thomas Byam Martin this innovation had not yet appeared in 1790.[110] The earliest example that I have been able to trace was in an order of 1798 that a number of 64-gun ships and some smaller, which were being fitted as transports, should each have a launch, with a jolly boat to stow inside it on the spar-deck, and two 25ft cutters which were to 'hang' at davits on each quarter.[111] By 1804 the fitting of davits was becoming common. The quarters of some ships were of unsuit-

2ème position de fin de combat du Vau français le Formidable de 80 can
de 80 canons, le Vénérable et le Superbe de 74 canons et la frégate la
à deux lieues dans le S. O. de l'île Saint-Pedro, près de Cadix.

, commandé par le Cap.ne Troude contre les V.aux anglais le César
mise de 56 canons , le 23 Messidor , an 9. (12 Juillet 1801)
e matin beau tems).

P. OZANNE, delineavit.

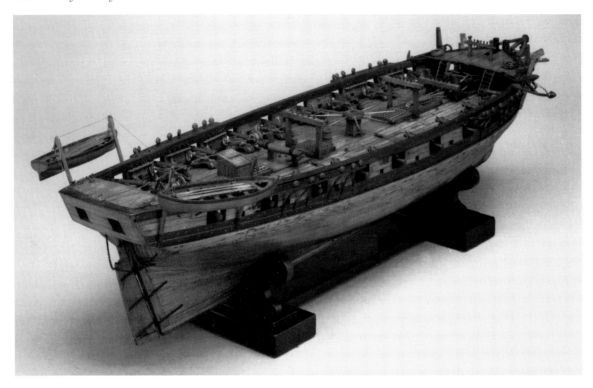

Above Quarter davits, as demonstrated by this model of a *Cruizer* class brig sloop of about 1805, gave the advantages not only of quick release, but also of clearing the deck of at least some of the boats. Davits were simple balks of timber hinged at one end and were incapable of hoisting the heavier boats, so were usually confined to clinker-built cutters, although this model has a double-ended boat under the starboard davit. This is probably one of the 'whale-gigs' which became popular towards the end of the Napoleonic Wars. (*SLR0348/D4072D*)

able form for them and in these a single pair of davits was fitted so that a boat could be hoisted across the stern.

On 2 January 1805 the Admiralty issued an instruction that davits were not to be fitted in vessels that were smaller than sloops.[112] It was thought to be dangerous. Nevertheless, the order seems to have been largely forgotten for in 1822 it was found that many small vessels had been fitted with them and when the Navy Board proposed to remove them the captains of the ships concerned were rather justifiably annoyed. The original davits had been straight wooden timbers, but in the 1820s curved davits of iron were beginning to come in.

Previous pages The frigate *Thames* launching her boats to go to the assistance of the dismasted *Venerable* during Saumarez's defeat of the Franco-Spanish squadron, 12 July 1801. Not often depicted, this operation is shown in meticulous detail by the French marine artist Pierre Ozanne. Even heaved-to in calm conditions as here, it required skilful seamanship, but in less ideal circumstances boats were often damaged or lost, providing a real incentive to the development of davits. (*C8722-A*)

Dimensions of boats, about 1705

LONGBOATS

Long	Broad	Deep	Oars
Feet	Ft-ins	Ft-ins	No
34	9-10	3-9	10
33	9-7	3-8	10
32/31	9-0	3-6	10
30	8-5	3-5½	10
29	8-2	3-5	8
28	7-8	3-5	7
27	7-6	3-5	7
26	7-4	3-4	7
25/24	7-2	3-1	6
23/22	7-0	3-0	6

PINNACES

Long	Broad	Deep	Oars
Feet	Ft-ins	Ft-ins	No
32	6-2	2-6½	10
32/31	6-1	2-6	10
29	6-0	2-6	9
28	5-11	2-5½	8
26/25	5-8	2-4	8
24/23/22	5-10	2-5	6

YAWLS

Long	Broad	Deep	Oars
Feet	Ft-ins	Ft-ins	No
27	6-4	2-7	8
23	6-0 or 5-9	2-5	6
21	5-8	2-2	6

The Yawls section also includes lengths of 26ft, 25ft, 24ft, 22ft, 20ft, 19ft, 18ft and 17ft but with no other details.

From a shipwright's notebook of about 1705, NMM CLU/6.

Scantlings of boats, about 1705

		LONGBOATS						PINNACES			YAWLS	
Boat lengths (feet)		35/34	33/32	32/30	29/28	27-25	24-21	35-31	30-26	25-21	24-21	20-17
Keel	Deep	7	6½	6	5½	5	4	4½	4	3½	3½	3¼
	Broad	6	5½	5	4½	4	3½	4	3½	3	3	2¾
Stem	Thick	5	5	4½	4	3½	3¼	3½	3	3	3	2½
	Broad	8	7	7	6½	6	5½	6	5½	4½	4½	4
Post, fore & aft	Aloft	5	4½	4½	4	3½	3	3½	3	2½	2½	2
	Alow	12	10	9½	9½	9	8½	10	10	9½	9½	9
Post, thwart		5	4½	4	3¾	3½	3	3	3	2½	2½	2¼
Board (thick)	Wainscott	1¼	1¼	1¼	1¼	1	1	1	1	1	1	¾
	Upper strake	1	1	1	1	1	1	¾	¾	¾	¾	¾
Thwarts (thick)	Main	4	3½	3½	3½	3	2½	2	2	2	2	1½
	Loose	2	2	2	2	1½	1½	1½	1½	1½	1½	1½
Gunwales	Thick	3	3	3	3	3	2½	1½	1½	1½	1½	1¼
	Deep	4½	4	4	3½	3¼	3	4½	4	3½	3½	3¼
Risings	Thick	1½	1½	1¼	1¼	1¼	1	1	1	¾	¾	¾
	Broad	7	6½	6	6	5½	5	4	4	3½	3½	3½
Footwaling	Thick	1½	1½	1¼	1¼	1¼	1	1	1	¾	¾	¾
	Broad	7	6½	6	6	5½	5	4	4	3½	3½	3½
Kelson	Thick	3	3	2½	2½	2	2	1½	1½	1½	1½	1½
	Broad	10	10	9½	9	8½	8	8	7	6½	6½	6

Boat lengths (feet)		LONGBOATS						PINNACES			YAWLS	
		35/34	33/32	32/30	29/28	27–25	24–21	35–31	30–26	25–21	24–21	20–17
Timbers	Thick	2 ¾	2 ½	2 ½	2 ½	2 ¼	2	1 ½	1 ½	1 ½	1 ½	1 ¼
	In & out	2 ½	1 ¼	2 ¼	2	2	1 ¾	1 ½	1 ½	1 ½	1 ½	1 ¼
Distance	or room	11	12	12	12	12	12	11 ½	11	11	11	10 ½
Wales	Thick	3	3	3	3	2 ½	2 ½	--	--	--	--	--
	Deep	4	4	3 ¾	3	3	3 ¾	--	--	--	--	--
Scarfs of timbers		30	30	30	28	26	26	24	20	20	20	18
Windlass square		11	10	10	9	8	7 ½	--	--	--	--	--

Dimensions in inches. From a shipwright's notebook of about 1705, NMM CLU/6.

Proportions of boats, about 1745

To find the proportions of a pinnace

Let the length of the keel be what it will, the proportionable breadth for a short boat is ¼ of the length of the keel, but for a long pinnace you must allow ⅕ or ⅙ and for the depth allow an inch to every foot of the length, the height of the sheer afore and abaft is ¾ of the breadth and the transom 6 inches above that. But if the boat be very long let the depth be ⅞ of an inch to every foot of the length, raking stern ½ the breadth and the post a quarter of its length, breadth of the transom ⅔ or ¾ of the main breadth. Length of the hancing to be ⅓ of the length of the boat; as for the rising and height of breadth place them as you please; to find the place of the midship flat, set off ⁸⁄₁₅ of the length of the boat from abaft.

Rules for finding longboats' length and breadth

For the breadth as you increase one foot in length so increase 3 inches in breadth, for the depth from 30 to 36 foot as you increase one foot in length so increase one inch in depth. Line ⁵⁄₁₄ from afore, the sheer 4 inches to a foot, and from 24 to 30 [foot length] ¾ of an inch in depth [the wording of this sentence is obscure, but the first part possibly means the maximum breadth is ⁵⁄₁₄ of the length from forward]

LONGBOATS			PINNACES		
Length	*Breadth*	*Depth*	*Length*	*Breadth*	*Depth*
Feet	Ft–ins	Ft–ins	Feet	Ft–ins	Ft–ins
36	10–3	4–4			
35	10–0	4–3	34	6–3	2–7
34	9–9	4–2			
33	9–6	4–1			
32	9–3	4–0	32 (10-oared)	6–2	2–6 ½
31	9–0	3–11			
30	8–9	3–10			
29	8–6	3–9 ¼	29	5–10	2–5
28	8–3	3–8 ½	28 (8-oared)	5–10	2–5
27	8–0	3–7 ¾			
26	7–9	3–7			
25	7–6	3–6 ¼			
24	7–3	3–5 ½			
			18 yawl	5–10	2–4

The dimensions above are by the Navy Board Warrant in April 1740: all 10-oared boats to be 32 foot long and 8-oared boats to be 28 foot long. Also 1st, 2nd and 3rd Rates to have an additional boat 25 foot long to row with 6 oars and built in the manner of Deal yawls of 18 foot; yawls of 21 foot fitted with a trunk, of 18 [foot] with 4 oars for a 40-gun ship.

Boat's mast

The mast must be 3 times the breadth of the boat in feet . . . the foremast if any to be ⅕ of the mainmast. The diameter is $\frac{7}{10}$ of an inch to a yard, the spreet a foot longer and about ⅔ of an inch to a yard.

Shoulder of mutton sails

The mast to be 4 times the breadth of the boat, diameter ⅔ of an inch to a yard in length, allowing ¾ of the length of the mast for the length of the boom; for diameter $\frac{5}{7}$ of an inch to a yard of length at the biggest end and at the small end ½ the biggest end. where you fay the back the length of the gaff $\frac{1}{6}$ of the boom.

From the manuscript notebook of William Wilkins, a shipwright at Chatham Dockyard, about 1745; NMM SPB/20. Spelling and punctuation modernised.

Boat establishments 1670–1800 (read across)

DATE	RATES						
	First	*Second*	*Third*	*Fourth*	*Fifth*	*Sixth*	*Sloops, etc*
About 1670	3 boats: longboat pinnace yawl	3 boats 70 and above; 2 boats	2 boats: longboat pinnace below 70s	2 boats: longboat pinnace	2 boats: longboat pinnace	4 largest vessels had 2 boats; all others 1 only; pinnace	
1679		*Duchess*, 90 guns 32ft longboat 31ft pinnace 20ft skiff (yawl)					
1701				3rd boat added: 60s a 6-oared, and 50s a 4-oared Deal yawl			
1702	Extra carvel Deal yawl-type boat [total 4 boats]	*Ditto* total: 90s probably 4 boats 80s probably 3 boats	*Ditto* total: 3 boats	total 3 boats	total 2 boats	total 1 boat	
After 1715	Tendency for the longboats issued to become shorter particularly in smaller ships						
1715						2nd boat added – 27ft pinnace 17ft yawl	
17/4/1740 [1]	Additional 25ft 6-oared boat, or Deal cutter	*Ditto*	*Ditto*: also in 70s the 10-oared boat [longboat] be lengthened to 32ft like the larger ships, and the 8-oared boat [pinnace?] to be 28ft	No change in numbers, but boats of 60s and 50s to be altered like the 70s			
	[total 5 boats]	[total 5 boats]	[total 3 boats]	[total 3 boats]			
11/7/1746 [2]				Additional 25ft cutter for 1745 Establishment 60s & 50s [total 4 boats]	*Ditto* for 44-gun ships of 1745 Establishment [total 3 boats]	[total 2 boats]	
9/4/1755 [3]	Additional Deal cutter [total 6 boats]	*Ditto* [total 6 boats]	*Ditto* [total 5 boats]				
19/8/1757 [4]						All 6th rates on Channel Service have a 6-oared boat in lieu of 10-oared boat [pinnace?]	
1761				36s and 32s: 23ft longboat 30ft pinnace 24ft yawl	28s: 22ft longboat 28ft pinnace 23ft yawl 24s: 21ft longboat 28ft pinnace 22ft yawl	16s: 19ft longboat 26ft pinnace 18s: 18ft longboat 25ft pinnace 10s: 16ft longboat 24ft pinnace	
				[total 3 boats]	[total 3 boats]	[total 2 boats]	

DATE	RATES						
	First	*Second*	*Third*	*Fourth*	*Fifth*	*Sixth*	*Sloops, etc*
1771			74s: longboat, pinnace, barge, yawl and 2 cutters of different lengths [total 6 boats]				
1777							16s of more than 300 tons given an extra 18ft 4-oared cutter
1779 [5]							Cutters and brigs on the establishment of sloops to have a 4-oared yawl or cutter
1780			64s: 30ft launch 32ft and 28ft pinnaces two 25ft cutters [total 5 boats]	38s: 26ft launch 30ft pinnace two 24ft cutters [total 4 boats]			
12/7/1780 [5]				36s: to have two 24ft cutters as 38s			
7/11/1780 [5]	Launches ordered to replace longboats in all vessels being built or repaired						
14/6/1781 [5]	An additional 4-oared 18ft cutter for all rates down to and including 20s						
1781 [7]			74s: 31ft launch 32ft & 28ft pinnaces two 25ft cutters one 18ft cutter 64s: 30ft launch 32ft and 28ft pinnaces [total 7 boats]	50s: 29ft launch pinnace (?30ft) two cutters (probably 25ft) 18ft cutter two 25ft and one [total 7 boats]	44s: 26ft launch pinnace (?30ft) two cutters (probably 24ft) 18ft cutter 36s and 32s: 23ft/24ft launch 30ft pinnace 18ft cutter [total 6 boats]	28s: 22ft launch 28ft pinnace 22ft cutter (?) 18ft cutter 20s: 21ft launch pinnace ?22ft 18ft cutter two 24ft cutters [total 5 boats]	large sloops: 19ft launch 26ft pinnace and probably 18ft cutter small sloops: 24ft and 16ft cutter 18ft cutter [total 5 boats]
[*Scout* purchased]							
[total 3/4 boats]	[total 3/2 boats]						
1782-3	Tendency to replace barges and pinnaces with cutters (preferred by many sea officers)						
1782 [5]							Fireships to have a 6-oared cutter in lieu of 6-oared boat [yawl?]
24/6/1783 [6]							Cutters to have two boats instead of one
9/7/1783 [6]							Large sloops of 300+ tons to be allowed a 28ft pinnace in lieu of 26ft boat
1/8/1783 [6]				60-32 gun ships to have a barge instead of present 30ft boat (pinnace?)			
4/9/1783 [6]							Cutters employed against smugglers to have 20ft boat instead of 18ft for duration of the peace
12/1/1784 [6]						28s allowed a 30ft pinnace instead of 28ft	

1794 A few captains allowed 8-oared cutters in lieu of pinnaces by special order

References not given in the text: [1] Adm/A/2282, 17 Apr 1740 [2] Adm/B/150, 11 Jul 1746 [3] Adm/B/150, 9 Apr 1755 [4] Adm/B/156, 19 Aug 1757 [5] Adm/106/2508, 1779, 7 Nov 1780, 14 Jun 1781, 24 Jun 1782 [6] Adm/106/2509, 1783, 17 Jul, 1 Aug, 4 Sep 1783, 1784. [7] Compiled from Adm/106/2508

The dimensions and scantlings of boats, about 1800

Particulars, etc	Species	Longboats										Launches							
	Lengths	32 feet		30 feet		26 feet		22 feet		19 feet		36 feet		33 feet		30 feet		24 feet	
		ft.	in.	ft.	in.	ft.	in.	ft.	in.	ft.	in.	ft.	in	ft.	in.	ft.	in.	ft.	in.
Breadth	Moulded	9	6	9	3	8	9	7	6	7	1	10	6	9	9	9	0	7	10
Depth	in midships	4	3	4	1	3	8	3	6	2	10	4	3	4	0	3	10	3	3
	afore	5	6	3	4	4	9	4	2	3	3	5	0	4	9	4	6	3	9
	abaft	5	7	3	5	4	10	4	3	3	4	5	0	4	9	4	6	3	9
Keel	Sided in midships	0	5½	0	5	0	4¾	0	E	0	3¼	0	7	0	6½	0	6	0	5½
	Deep below the rabbet	0	6½	0	6	0	5¾	0	5¾	0	5	0	5	0	5	0	5	0	4½
	To be above the rabbet																		
	for deadwood	0	1¼	0	1	0	0⅞	0	0¾	0	0¼	0	0½	0	1¼	0	1¼	0	1
Stem	Sided	0	4½	0	4	0	3⅞	0	3¼	0	3½	0	5¼	0	5⅛	0	5	0	4¾
	Afore rabbet at head	0	7	0	6½	0	6	0	5½	0	5	0	5¼	0	5⅛	0	5	0	4½
	Abaft the rabbet	0	1¾	0	1¾	0	1⅝	0	⅜	0	1⅜	0	2¾	0	2½	0	2½	0	2
Transom	Broad or moulded at																		
	the upper part	5	11	5	8	5	3	3	9	3	4	9	0	8	3	7	6	6	6
	Thick or sided	0	4	0	4	0	3½	0	3	0	2¼	0	4	0	3¾	0	3½	0	3
	Knees, sided	0	3½	0	3½	0	3¼	0	2¾	0	2	0	4	0	3¾	0	3½	0	3
Stern-post	Sided at the tuck	0	4¾	0	4½	0	3¾	0	3¼	0	3	0	5½	0	5¼	0	5	0	4¾
	Sided at the keel	0	3½	0	3¼	0	2¾	0	E	0	2½	0	5½	0	5¼	0	5	0	4¾
	Broad, fore and aft at keel	1	4	1	2	1	1	1	0	0	10	1	1	1	0	0	11	0	10
	[Transom included] at head	0	8¼	0	7½	0	6¼	0	5	0	4½	0	6¼	0	6	0	5¾	0	5¼
Floor-timbers	Sided	0	3	0	3	0	2¾	0	2½	0	1¾	0	4	0	3½	0	2¾	0	2¼
	Moulded at the head	0	3	0	3	0	2½	0	2¼	0	1⅝	0	3¾	0	3½	0	2¼	0	2¼
	Moulded at the throat	0	5¼	0	5	0	4½	0	4¼	0	3¾	0	6	0	5½	0	5	0	4½
Futtocks	Sided at the heel	0	3	0	2¼	0	2½	0	2⅛	0	1¾	0	4	0	3¾	0	3	0	2
	Sided at the heads	0	2¾	0	2¼	0	2	0	1⅞	0	1½	0	3½	0	3¼	0	2½	0	1½
	Moulded at the heads	0	2¾	0	2½	0	2	0	1⅞	0	1½	0	3½	0	3¼	0	2½	0	1½
	Scarph of the timbers	3	0	2	10	2	4	2	0	1	10	3	0	2	9	2	6	2	2
Keelson	Broad	1	1	1	0	1	0	0	11	0	10½	1	2	1	1	1	0	0	10
	Thick	0	3	0	3	0	2½	0	1¾	0	1½	0	3	0	2¾	0	2½	0	2
Footwaling	Thick	0	1¼	0	1¼	0	1	0	1	0	1	0	1½	0	1¼	0	1¼	0	1
Rising	Broad	0	10	0	10	0	9	0	8	0	6½	0	11	0	10	0	8½	0	7
	Thick	0	1¼	0	1¼	0	1½	0	1½	0	1	0	1	0	1¼	0	1⅛	0	1
Thwarts – Main	Broad	1	0	0	11	0	11	0	10	0	10	1	1	1	0	0	11	0	10
	Thick	0	4	0	3¾	0	3½	0	3¼	0	3	0	4	0	3¾	0	3½	0	3¼

Barges		Pinnaces								Cutter								Yawls				Wherry	
37 feet		32 feet		28 feet		25 feet		17 feet		30 feet		25 feet		21 feet		16 feet		26 feet		16 feet		25 feet	
ft.	in.	ft.	in.	ft.	in.	ft.	in.	ft.	in.	ft.	in.	ft.	in.	ft.	in.	ft.	in.	ft.	in.	ft.	in.	ft.	in.
7	9	7	6	6	10	6	0	5	9	7	0	6	10	6	7	6	0	6	8	5	6	5	11
3	0	3	3	3	0	2	7	2	5	2	10	2	8	2	6	2	3	2	11	2	3½	2	4
3	10	4	0	3	8	3	2	2	11	3	8	3	3	3	1	2	9	3	6	2	9	30	½
4	3	4	4	4	0	3	5	3	2	3	9	3	4	3	1	2	9	3	9	2	11	2	11½
0	4¼	0	4½	0	4	0	3¾	0	3½	0	4	0	3¼	0	3½	0	3	0	3¾	0	3¼	0	3¼
0	5	0	5	0	4½	0	4	0	4	0	4	0	3½	0	3¼	0	2¾	0	3	0	2¾	0	3½
0	1	0	1	0	0⅞	0	0⅞	0	0¾	0	1	0	0⅞	0	0¾	0	0¾	0	0¾	0	0¾	0	0¾
0	4	0	4	0	3¾	0	3½	0	3¼	0	3½	0	3¼	0	3	0	2¾	0	3¼	0	2¾	0	2½
0	3½	0	3¾	0	3½	0	3¼	0	3	0	5	0	4¾	0	4½	0	4	0	4½	0	4	0	3½
0	2½	0	2½	0	2½	0	2¼	0	2⅛	0	1½	3	1⅜	0	1¼	0	1¼	0	1¼	0	1⅛	0	1¼
4	9	4	7	4	0	3	6	3	0	3	3	0	1	2	10	2	4	3	8	2	7	1	6
0	2½	0	2½	0	2¼	0	2	0	1¾	0	1¾	0	1½	0	1½	0	1¼	0	1¾	0	1½	0	1½
iron		iron		iron		iron		iron		0	1¾	0	1½	0	1½	0	1¼	iron		iron		iron	
0	3¾	0	3½	0	3¼	0	3	0	2¾	0	3	0	2⅞	0	2¾	0	2½	0	2⅝	0	2¼	0	2¾
0	3¼	0	3	0	2¾	0	2½	0	2⅜	0	2½	0	2½	0	2⅜	0	2	0	2¼	0	1¾	0	2¼
0	11½	0	11	0	10	0	9¼	0	8½	0	9	0	9	0	8½	0	7	0	8¾	0	7	0	8
0	3	0	2¾	0	2½	0	2¼	0	2	0	4	0	4	0	3¾	0	3	0	2	0	1½	0	3¼
0	1¾	0	1¾	0	1⅝	0	1½	0	1⅜	0	1¾	0	1½	0	1⅜	0	1¼	0	1¾	0	1½	0	1
0	1¾	0	1¾	0	1⅝	0	1⅜	0	1¼	0	1⅝	0	1¼	0	1¼	0	1⅛	0	1⅝	0	1½	0	1¼
0	4	0	4	0	3¾	0	3⅝	0	3½	0	3	0	2¾	0	2⅜	0	2	0	3½	0	3	0	2¾
0	1¾	0	1½	0	1½	0	1⅜	0	1¼	0	1½	0	1⅜	0	1¼	0	1⅛	0	1½	0	1¼	0	1
0	1¼	0	1¼	0	1¼	0	1¼	0	1⅛	0	1¼	0	1⅛	0	1	0	0⅞	0	1¼	0	1⅛	0	1
0	1¼	0	1¼	0	1¼	0	1¼	0	1⅛	0	1¾	0	1⅛	0	1	0	0⅞	0	1¼	0	1⅛	0	1
2	0	1	10	1	9	1	8	1	7	2	0	1	10	1	9	1	7	1	10	1	8	1	8
0	11	0	11	0	11	0	10½	0	10	0	10	0	9½	0	9½	0	8	0	10	0	9	0	10
0	1¼	0	1¼	0	1⅛	0	1⅛	0	1⅛	0	1¼	0	1⅛	0	1	0	0⅞	0	1⅛	0	1	0	1⅛
0	0¾	0	0¾	0	0¾	0	0¾	0	0⅝	0	0¾	0	0¾	0	0¾	0	0⅝	0	0¾	0	0¾	0	0¾
0	4½	0	4½	0	4½	0	4⅛	0	4	0	4	0	4	0	3¾	0	3½	0	6	0	5	0	3½
0	0⅞	0	0⅞	0	0⅞	0	0⅞	0	0⅞	0	0⅞	0	0⅞	0	0⅞	0	0¾	0	1	0	1	0	0⅞
0	10	0	10	0	10	0	9½	0	9	0	10	0	9	0	8	0	7	0	10	0	9	0	9¼
0	1½	0	1½	0	1½	0	1½	0	1½	0	1½	0	1½	0	1½	0	1⅜	0	1¾	0	1⅝	0	1¼

The Boats of Men-of-War

Species	Particulars, etc	Longboats 32 feet		30 feet		26 feet		22 feet		19 feet		Launches 36 feet		33 feet		30 feet		24 feet	
	Lengths	ft.	in.	ft.	in.	ft.	in.	ft.	in.	ft.	in.	ft.	in	ft.	in.	ft.	in.	ft.	in.
Thwarts – After	Broad	0	9	0	9	0	9	0	9	0	9	0	9	0	9	0	9	0	9
	Thick	0	2½	0	2½	0	2½	0	2¼	0	2	0	2½	0	2½	0	2¼	0	2
Thwarts – Fore	Broad	0	10	0	10	0	10	0	10	0	10	0	9	0	9	0	9	0	9
	Thick	0	2¾	0	2¾	0	2½	0	2½	0	2¼	0	2¼	0	2½	0	2¼	0	2
Thwarts – Loose	Broad	0	9	0	9	0	8	0	8	0	8	0	9	0	9	0	9	0	9
	Thick	0	2	0	2	0	2	0	1¼	0	1½	0	2½	0	2½	0	2¼	0	2
	Knees on the thwarts, sided	0	3	0	3	0	2¼	0	2½	0	2¼	0	4	0	3¾	0	3½	0	3
Benches	Broad	1	0	1	0	1	0	0	11	0	11	1	0	1	0	1	0	1	0
	Thick	0	1½	0	1½	0	1½	0	1¾	0	1¼	0	1½	0	1½	0	1½	0	1½
Deadwood	Sided	0	3½	0	3¼	0	2¼	0	2¼	0	2	0	4½	0	4	0	3½	0	3
Bottom	Thick	0	1⅛	0	1⅛	0	1⅛	0	1	0	0⅞	0	1½	0	1¼	0	1⅛	0	0⅞
Landing strake	Broad	0	11	0	10½	0	9½	0	9	0	8¾	0	11	0	10	0	9	0	8
Upper strake	Broad	1	0	0	11½	0	10	0	9	0	8	1	0	0	11	0	10	0	9
Gunwale	Deep	0	3¾	0	3½	0	3	0	2½	0	2¼	0	4¼	0	4¼	0	3¼	0	3
	Thick	0	4	0	3¾	0	3¼	0	2½	0	2	0	4	0	4	0	3½	0	3¼
Breasthook	Sided	0	3½	0	3	0	2½	0	2¼	0	2	0	4	0	4	0	3½	0	3
	Length	4	6	4	2	3	6	3	2	2	10	5	0	4	3	3	9	3	0
	Moulded at the throat	0	7	0	6	0	5	0	4½	0	4	0	10	0	9	0	7	0	5
Ears	Sided	0	3¾	0	3½	0	3¼	0	3	0	2½	0	4	0	3¾	0	3½	1	3
	Length	1	9	1	8	1	6	1	4	1	2	2	0	1	10	1	9	0	6
Chocks	Thick	0	3¼	0	3	0	2¾	0	2½	0	2	0	4½	0	3½	0	3	1	2½
	Length	1	6	1	5	1	4	1	2	1	1	3	0	2	9	1	4	0	2
Washboards	Broad bow / quarter	0	7	0	7	0	7	0	6	0	5¼	0	6	0	6	0	6	0	6
Bowsprit step	Thick	0	3	0	3	0	2½	iron		iron									
	Broad	1	2½	1	2	1	0	iron		iron									
Windlass	Diameter	0	10	0	9½	0	9	0	8	0	7	0	11	0	10	0	9	0	8
Chocks	Thick	0	6	0	5½	0	5	0	4½	0	4	0	6½	0	6	0	5½	0	5
	Broad	0	11	0	11	0	10	0	9	0	9	1	3	1	2	1	0	0	11
Rudder	Breadth at the heel	2	0	1	10	1	8	1	7	1	6	2	0	1	10	1	9	1	7
	Breadth at the hance	1	4¼	1	3½	1	2	1	1	1	0½	1	6	1	4	1	3	1	1½
	Breadth at the head	0	9	0	8½	0	8	0	7½	0	7	0	10	0	9	0	9	0	8
	Thickness	0	1½	0	1½	0	1¼	0	1¼	0	1¼	0	1⅜	0	1½	0	1½	0	1½

From David Steel, *The Elements and Practice of Naval Architecture* (London 1805)

Barges 37 feet		Pinnaces 32 feet		Pinnaces 28 feet		Pinnaces 25 feet		Pinnaces 17 feet		Cutter 30 feet		Cutter 25 feet		Cutter 21 feet		Cutter 16 feet		Yawls 26 feet		Yawls 16 feet		Wherry 25 feet	
ft.	in.	ft.	in.	ft.	in.	ft.	in.	ft.	in.	ft.	in.	ft.	in.	ft.	in.	ft.	in.	ft.	in.	ft.	in.	ft.	in.
0	9	0	9	0	9	0	8½	0	8	0	8	0	8	0	8	0	7	0	7½	0	7	0	7½
0	1¾	0	1¾	0	1¾	0	1⅝	0	1½	0	1¾	0	1¾	0	1¾	0	1½	0	1½	0	1½	0	1¼
0	8	0	8	0	8	0	7½	0	7	0	10	0	10	0	10	0	9	0	7½	0	7	0	8½
0	8½	0	8½	0	1½	0	1⅜	0	1⅜	0	2	0	2	0	2	0	1¾	0	1½	0	1½	0	1⅛
0	8	0	8	0	8	0	7½	0	7	0	8	0	8	0	8	0	7	0	7½	0	7	0	7½
0	1½	0	1½	0	1½	0	1⅜	0	1¼	0	1¾	0	1½	0	1½	0	1½	0	1½	0	1½	0	1¼
iron		iron		iron		iron		iron		0	1¼	0	1⅛	0	1⅛	0	1	iron		iron		iron	
1	0	1	0	0	11	0	11	0	10	1	0	0	11	0	11	0	10	0	11	0	10	1	0
0	1¼	0	1¼	0	1¼	0	1⅛	0	1⅛	0	1¼	0	1¼	0	1¼	0	1⅛	0	1¼	0	1⅛	0	1⅛
0	3	0	3	0	2¾	0	2½	0	2½	0	2¾	0	2½	0	2½	0	2	0	2¼	0	2	0	2
0	0⅞	0	0⅞	0	0⅞	0	0⅞	0	0⅞	0	0¾	0	0¾	0	0⅝	0	0⅝	0	0⅞	0	0⅞	0	0¾
0	6½	0	6½	0	6½	0	6½	0	5	0	5½	0	5	0	4½	0	4	0	8	0	7½	0	6
0	6½	0	6½	0	6½	0	6½	0	5½	0	6	0	6	0	5	0	4½	0	8	0	7½	0	6½
0	3¾	0	3¾	0	3½	0	3½	0	3¼	0	2	0	1¾	0	1½	0	1½	0	2½	0	2¼	0	3¼
0	1¾			0	1½	0	1½	0	1½	0	2½	0	2¾	0	2	0	2	0	2	0	1¾	0	1½
0	1¾	0	1¾	0	1½	0	1½	0	1⅜	0	2¼	0	2	0	1¾	0	1½	0	2	0	1¾	0	1½
2	6	2	4	2	2	2	0	1	8	1	9	1	8	1	7	1	6	2	4	2	2	2	0
0	4	0	4	0	4	0	3½	0	3	0	3½	0	3	0	2¼	0	2½	0	3½	0	3	0	3
0	1¾	0	1¾	0	1⅝	0	1½	0	1½	0	1⅝	0	1½	0	1¼	0	1¼	0	2	0	1¾	0	1½
0	11	0	10	0	10	0	10	0	10	1	4	1	2	0	11	0	9	1	0	0	11	0	10
0	1½	0	1½	0	1¾	0	1¼	0	1¼	0	1½	0	1¼	0	1¼	0	1¼	0	1¼	0	1½	0	1¼
1	2	1	2	1	1	1	0	0	11	1	3	1	2	1	0	0	11	1	1	1	0	0	11
0	4½	0	4½	0	4½	0	4	0	3½	5	0	5	0	0	4½	0	4½	0	4½	0	4½	0	4½
0	5½	0	5½	0	5½	0	5	0	4½									0	5½	0	5½	0	5½
1	7	1	6	1	5	1	3	1	1	1	6	1	4	1	2½	1	1	1	5	1	3	1	3
1	3	1	2	1	1	1	0	0	10	1	2	1	1	1	0	0	10	1	0½	0	11	0	11
0	9	0	8	0	7½	0	7½	0	7½	0	7	0	7	0	6½	0	6	0	7	0	6	0	5
0	1⅛	0	1	0	1	0	1	0	0⅞	0	1	0	0⅞	0	0⅞	0	0⅞	0	0⅞	0	0⅞	0	0⅞

Boats carried, about 1815, with earlier amendments

Type of ship (no of guns)	Barge or 10-oared boat of length (ft)	Longboat or launch length (ft)	Pinnace length (ft)	Deal cutters length (ft)	4-oared Deal cutter, cutter or jolly boat length (ft)
100	32	34	28	25x2 [1]	18
98 or 90	32	33	28	25x2 [1]	18
80	32	32	28	25x2 [1]	18
74	32	31	28 [2]	25x2 [1]	18
64	32 [3]	30	28	25x2 [1]	18
50	32 [3]	29		25x2 [1]	18
44	32 [3]	26 [4]		25x2 [1]	18
40	32 [3]	26 [4]		25x2 [1]	18
38	32 [3]	26 [4]		25x2 [1]	18
36	32 [3]	25 [4]		25x2 [1]	18
32	30	23 [4,5]		24 [6]	18
28	28	22 [4]		24	18
24	28	21 [4]		Cutter 22 or yawl 26	18
20	28	21 [7]		22	18

	Longboat or launch	Pinnace or 6-oared cutter	Deal cutter	Pinnace	4-oared Deal cutter or yawl
Sloops of 361 tons plus	18 or 19 [8,9]			28 [8]	18 [10]
Sloops 268 to 341 tons	18 or 19 [8,9]			28 [8]	18 [8,10]
Brigs, 200 tons			24 & 20		16
Fireships	19 [8]		22 [8]		18
Bombs	19	25			18
Sloops, 200 tons	16 [4]			24 [8]	
Cutters			20 [11]		
Brigs, 158 tons			22 or 24		16 [12]

Notes:

1. To be allowed a yawl of 26ft in lieu of a cutter, on captains's application.

2. Or a 6-oared cutter.

3. To be allowed 8-oared cutter in lieu of barge, on captain's application.

4. In lieu of Brenton's yawl, Admiralty order, 15 March 1810.

5. NB, 32-gun ships carrying 18-pounders are to be allowed a launch of 25ft.

6. 18-pounder 32s also allowed Deal cutter of 25ft.

7. In lieu of 8-oared cutter, Admiralty order, 15 March 1810.

8. If rigged as a ship.

9. Sloops of 400 tons plus have launch or longboat of 2ft.

10. Sloops rigged as brigs of about 313 tons plus are allowed –

Cutter – 24ft	Brig sloops, 282 tons –
Cutter – 20ft	Cutter – 18ft
Cutter – 24ft	Cutter or jolly boat – 16ft.
Cutter or jolly boat – 16ft.	

11. The new cutters of 200 and 193 tons to have:
   Gig – 22ft
   Cutter – 16ft

12. Or a gig of 22ft.

From PRO Adm 7/579.

Chapter 3 NINETEENTH CENTURY DEVELOPMENTS

Apicture of the variety of types of boats available in the Royal Navy at the end of the French Wars can be obtained from the *Rate Book* for 1817.[113] This lists:

Launches	in 17 lengths, from 16ft to 34ft
Barges and Pinnaces	in 8 lengths, 28ft to 37ft
Cutters	in 17 lengths, 12ft to 34ft
Yawls	in 8 lengths, 16ft to 26ft
Galleys	30ft
Gigs	in 6 lengths, 18ft to 26ft
Life boats	in 6 lengths, 18ft to 30ft
Brenton's yawls	27ft
[a type of boat introduced in 1807; they were never popular]	
Wherries	23ft & 25ft

Long after the introduction of steam the majority of a big warship's boats continued to be sailing and pulling craft, and to be clearly descended from their eighteenth-century forebears. In this 1899 photograph the boats of a Channel Fleet battleship prepare for an all-comers race. The comparative sizes and proportions – not always obvious in individual draughts - are quite clear: the gig in the foreground, with a cutter beyond and the launch in the centre. (*59/1314*)

One of the reasons for retaining pulling and sailing boats after the introduction of steam was their value in inculcating the basic skills of the seaman in new officers and ratings alike. For the same reason the Royal Navy kept a squadron of sail-training brigs right down to the era of the *Dreadnought*. One of these, the *Nautilus*, is shown here about 1900; she has a galley or gig over the stern and steel davits for her quarter-boats, the port boat being a clinker-built cutter. (*N29463*)

The bracketing together of barges and pinnaces will be noted. At this period the only difference between them was that the barge should 'have Pannels and Mouldings fore and aft, but the Pinnace . . . should be pannelled only in the stern sheets.'[114]

Drawings of ship's boats, which might help in settling questions of build, are hard to come by. The National Maritime Museum has a fine collection from about 1780 onwards, but few before that time. Unfortunately a large number are undated so that they are not of great value in showing trends in design. The earliest are on a sheet dated 1709. An interesting point about this particular set is that only the yawls and a landing boat are named. The rest are described by the number of oars used. This confirms the view that there was little to choose between the barges and the pinnaces of this era and throughout the eighteenth century. The differences between them being minimal they are often only referred to by their lengths or the numbers of oars rowed.

The features of one type of boat tended to get transferred to another. Originally the oars were constrained between two round thole pins, pushed into holes in a block fastened inside the gunwale. When cutters were introduced these were made more seaworthy by the addition of an extra strake above the gunwale and rowlocks for the oars were cut in this strake. In the latter years of the eighteenth century barges, pinnaces and yawls were built in which the removable round thole pins were replaced by fixed vertical pieces of plank, edge on. Then removable wash-strakes were fitted between adjacent rowlocks and finally, as in the cutters, a permanent wash-strake was fitted along the whole length of the boat and had rowlocks cut in it. This development is clearly shown if one compares the drawings of boats made by Falconer in 1769 and by Burney in 1815.[115]

In 1826 Lieutenant Henry Mangles Denham, commanding the *Linnet*, introduced swivelling crutches. These had many advantages. If the looms of the oars were let go the oars trailed back fore-and-aft, thus avoiding damage and inconvenience, and their use was found to give a smoother motion to the stroke, which was a great advantage when surveying.[116] He was allowed to have all the boats of the *Linnet* so fitted, and apparently the idea was a success, for ultimately swivelling crutches were adopted for all single-banked boats.

Another development which came in gradually was in the shape of the bow. The drawings of 1709 show boats having a very full, almost semi-circular, bow. The advent of the cutter introduced a finer form and this design was followed by the barge and pinnace so that at the beginning of the nineteenth century only the launch, which had replaced the longboat, exhibited the very bluff bow. Later in the century, when the advent of steam had reduced the need to bring off vast quantities of water from the shore and

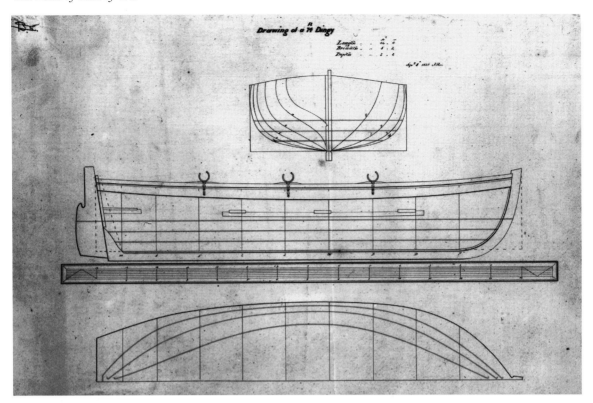

stowage for casks was no longer so important, the launch followed the same trend and sacrificed roominess to seaworthiness.

The plans of three 28ft pinnaces appear to show a development. In 1799 they had a beam of 6ft 4in and rowed eight oars, single-banked. In 1811 the beam had increased to 7ft, which allowed the oars to be double-banked so that they rowed sixteen. By 1852 the beam had gone up to 8ft 4in but the number of oars had been reduced to twelve.

At the end of the seventeenth century it was usual for the boats of men-of-war to be carvel-built, *ie* with their planking laid edge to edge; except when they were built at Deal, where the practice was for them to be clencher- (or clinker-) built with the lower edge of each plank overlapping the upper edge of the one below. Since yawls were usually built at Deal it followed that they were clinker-built. When the Royal yards started building yawls these were carvel-built, and both types remained in service side by side. The next departure at Deal was the building of cutters, and these also were clinker-built as were the gigs which were Deal's next introduction. When these two types began to be built in the yards this distinctive type of build was retained, though cutters were occasionally carvel-built.

When building a clinker-built boat the nails should be sufficiently long to be driven right through both planks, the ends being then clenched (or bent over) to prevent the nails working out. Clinker-built boats were always

A draught dated 8 September 1835 of a 14ft dinghy, a new type in the nineteenth-century Navy. This example shows the swivelling crutches introduced in 1826. (Bu(g)2)

lighter, more tender and more difficult to repair than carvel-built. It seems probable that the boatbuilders often economised by using nails which were too short to clench properly and that in consequence they worked out.

The comparative fraility of clinker-built boats and the difficulty of repairing them led in 1769 to an order that yawls for foreign-going vessels should be carvel-built and that clinker-built yawls should be restricted to Channel service.[117] In 1783 it was noted that when clinker-built boats had been allowed to go on foreign service they tended to become 'nail sick' and it was said that the trouble could be avoided if they were copper fastened instead of iron nails being used.[118] Nevertheless in 1800 it was decided that the only cutters to be sent abroad should be jollyboats.[119] In 1803 a Mr Boswell designed a boat with two skins for strength. The inner was to be clinker-built and the outer carvel.[120] The Royal Navy does not appear to have shown any interest at this time.

In 1820 the *Creole* was supplied for experiment with two quarter-boats which had carvel-built bottoms and clinker-built upperworks. Captain Alexander Mackenzie reported on them most enthusiastically, because though heavier than the usual clinker-built boats they were stronger and more easily kept in repair.[121] It was probably a result of this report that in the 1820s there was a considerable vogue for pure carvel-built boats. Officers were frequently asking that they might have carvel-built cutters instead of clinker-built. In 1823 Captain Thomas Wolrige of the *Driver*, a sloop on the West Coast of Africa, reported most strongly in favour of a carvel-built yawl which had been sent to him for trial.[122]

However, the demand for carvel-built cutters did not last and in 1831 Captain John Duff Markland of the *Briton* complained that the 23ft cutters supplied to his ship were useless, as they would neither row nor sail. It then transpired that carvel-built cutters had been constructed by mistake in 1830 and that these had been foisted upon the *Briton* by the dockyard because she did not immediately complain.[123] Again in 1836 we find Captain Maurice Frederick Fitzhardinge Berkeley of the *Hercules* complaining that she had been supplied with carvel-built cutters as quarter-boats and that these were more than a ton heavier than were clinker-built boats.[124]

In 1818 John Cow, the Master Boatbuilder at Woolwich, began to make a series of proposals for improvements in the methods of building launches and pinnaces, and in the method of mounting carronades in boats. Trials proceeded and in the early 1820s a number of officers were asking that their ships might have boats built on Cow's plan. There is some confusion about this. Cow had actually three proposals. The first was in the method of building boats; the second dealt with arrangements for transporting anchors and other heavy weights, such as guns; the third covered the means of mounting boat guns.

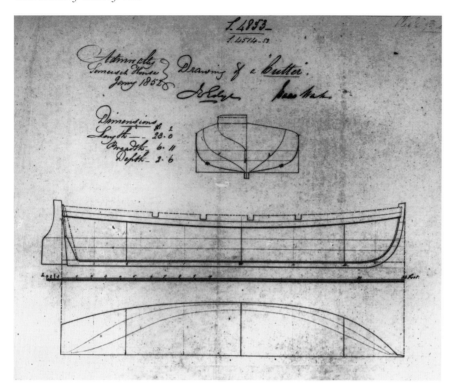

His design of launches proved unsatisfactory. One of them was supplied to the *Creole* for trial in 1820 and in 1822 Captain Thomas White, while approving the arrangements for handling anchors, reported that the boat was inclined to be crank and was so high out of the water that the oars could only be handled with difficulty. Reducing the height of the topsides improved matters, but the boat was still considered to be unsafe to hoist out at sea.[125]

Mr Cow's designs are described in his book.[126] For transporting heavy weights, two trunks, or tubes, were fitted just abaft the mid-point of the length of the boat and these allowed ropes from the anchor to be passed up through the bottom of the boat and brought to the windlass at thwart level just above them. By this means an anchor or gun could be hoisted close up under the boat, being steadied by ropes from it led inboard through rowlocks. If a field gun were suspended underneath her in this way, the boat could be brought close in-shore until the wheels of the gun-carriage grounded. The slings could then be cast off and the gun run up the beach. The boat would never have to take the ground, which might be of considerable advantage if there was any sea. Trials were carried out by the *Beagle* and *Cyrene* in 1825 and it was decided that one boat in each ship should be fitted in this manner.[127]

In 1828 Captain Hon George Elliot produced a new method of carrying heavy weights by boats. In a trial by the *Ganges* laying out an 84cwt

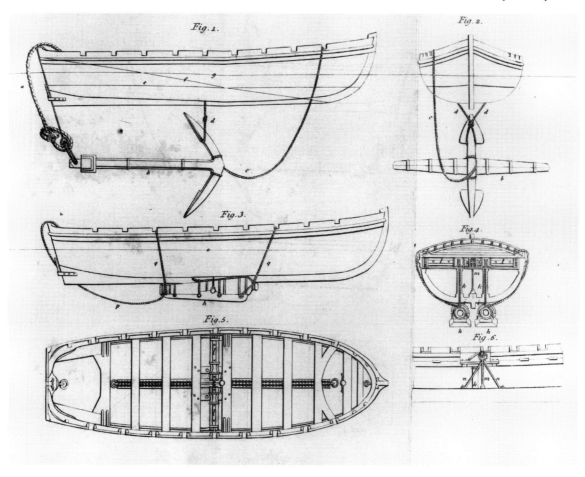

Fig. 1. Fig. 2. Fig. 3. Fig. 4. Fig. 5. Fig. 6.

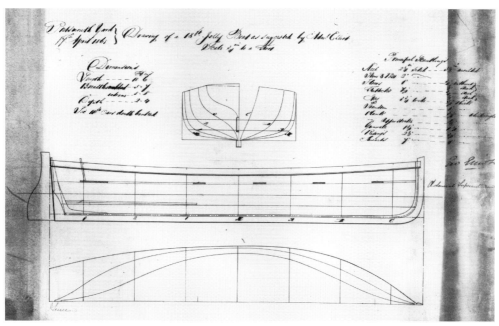

anchor the spindle of the windlass of a Cow launch broke, while the anchor was weighed without any difficulty by an Elliot launch from the *Victory*.[128] After a further comparative trial in 1830, in the following year the Admiralty decided that captains should have the choice of Cow or Elliot launches for their ships, and instructed the Navy Board to keep launches of both types in store. The Navy Board pointed out that the fitting of a boat on either plan was a simple matter and that it had always been the custom that launches in store should not have these fittings but should have them added as and when required.[129]

In 1826 Mr William Johns, Foreman in Plymouth Dockyard, designed a boat with two skins, in which the planking was arranged diagonally so that the planks of the two skins crossed each other at right angles. This scheme was found most effective and was adopted for launches and pinnaces, but considered too heavy for smaller boats. In 1840 Mr Johns was awarded £300 for his invention.[130] A Frenchman, La Fouche, unsuccessfully claimed priority of design.[131]

NEW BOAT TYPES

The nineteenth century was an era of great technological advancement, accompanied as far as the Royal Navy was concerned by demands for great economy. Apostles of progress might rail at naval officers for being slow in going over from sail to steam, but when steamships were built they were still expected to proceed under sail as much as possible to economise on the cost of coal. The Admiralty set up a committee to advise on the best compasses for iron ships and, when its report was received, restricted the use of the new compasses to a few ships on grounds of the high price of the new instruments. In consequence of this attitude material had to remain in use long after it was obsolete and thus there was a great lack of homogenity in any sphere.

The introduction of steam when it did come had a considerable effect on ships' boats, apart from their propulsion. The most important duties of boats had always been those of watering and of laying out or weighing anchors. For these every ship had had a longboat, later replaced by a launch, designed to carry as much water as possible without being too large for the ship. This need led to the provision of very many sizes of launch, each tailored for its own build of ship. Now steam brought with it the boon of a ship being able to distil water. Watering ship became less important. The greater mobility conferred by steam propulsion almost entirely removed the need for anchor work by boats. In consequence a smaller number of boat lengths could be standardised and the ship supplied when a boat was

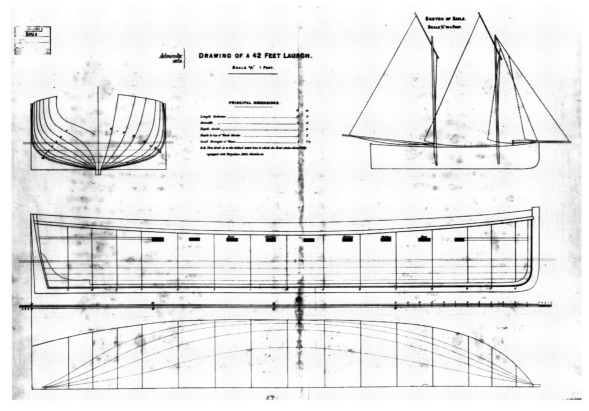

By the second half of the nineteenth century there was only one size of launch, a 42ft model. This 1878 draught shows the form and sail plan. It is one of a series of identical style draughts of different boat types all dated 1878 which probably represent the standard designs. *(Bu(a)93b)*

required with the next size below the optimum lengh that could be stowed. Thus through the century one sees a gradual decline in the number of lengths of pulling boats. The following appear in the *Rate Books*:

	1817	*1877*	*1900*	*1914*
Launch	7 lengths 16–34ft	1 length 42ft	1 length 42ft	1 length 42ft
Pinnace	8 lengths 28–37ft	5 lengths 25–32ft	4 lengths 28–36ft	3 lengths 30–36ft
Barge	8 lengths 28–37ft	5 lengths 28–36ft		
Cutter & Jollyboat	17 lengths 12–34ft	11 lengths 16–34ft	11 lengths 16–34ft	5 lengths 26–34ft
Yawl	8 lengths 16–26ft			
Galley	1 length 30ft			1 length 32ft
Gig	6 lengths 18–26ft	10 lengths★ 18–32ft	7 lengths 20–32ft	3 lengths 24–30ft
Skiff & Dinghy		2 lengths 12–14ft	5 lengths 10–16ft	3 lengths 10–16ft

(★Galleys and whalers were included in this figure. In 1900 and 1914 there were two lengths of whalers, 25ft and 27ft.)

A model of a late nineteenth century admiral's barge, with the officer's flag painted on the bow. (*SLR 1779/B9890*)

Sheer draught of a 34ft admiral's barge of 1878. The ringbolts on the kelson for the hoisting tackles are indicated. (*Bu(d)5b*)

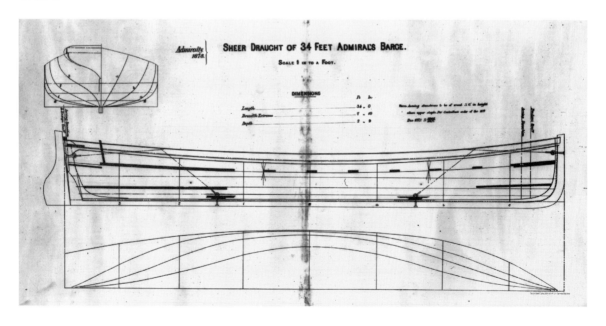

During the century new types of boats appeared and others gradually dropped out of use. The yawl disappeared in the 1830s, having been displaced by the cutter and jollyboat. The latter struggled on until 1882-3 when it made its last appearance in the *Rate Book*. By 1860 the barge, which had finally become exclusively the boat of flag officers, had become a clinker-built boat and thus completely divorced from the pinnace, the latter becoming a small version of the launch. The oared barge was finally displaced by a steam one and disappeared about 1893.

In 1825 the **dinghy** and shortly afterwards the **skiff** put in an appearance. These were small boats of 12ft or so which were convenient for harbour use in fine weather when only one or two officers or men needed to be transported. The name dinghy is of Indian origin and the type of boat as used in this country probably originated in East Indiamen. The earliest reference in the English language is in 1794.[132]

About the same time the **whaleboat** was introduced into the Royal Navy. Originally these boats were evolved in ships employed in whaling where, when attacking a whale, the greatest manoeuvreability was a prime consideration. Since the boat had to be able to be backed away from a whale with considerable rapidity the boat had a pointed stern like the original Norway yawls. The earliest use of the name was in 1756.[133] These boats were found to be very useful in the conditions of surf encountered by vessels

The Royal Navy's first double-ended boats were called 'whale-gigs' and were introduced towards the end of the Napoleonic Wars. They were designed as boarding boats, so from the beginning they were meant to be unsinkable. This is a highly developed version as repaired in 1879, a 24ft boat with the 'outside air cased' principle of floatation (buoyancy chambers along the inside of the hull) which illustrates their dual role as lifeboats as well. (*Bu(m)8*)

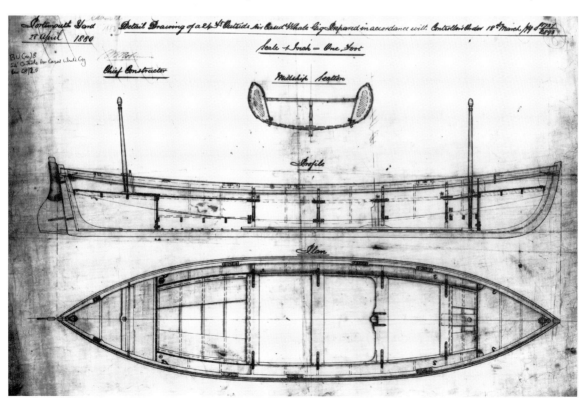

cruising for slavers off the west coast of Africa. Then they were found to be an excellent alternative to the gig for other ships and their use rapidly spread. Whaleboats soon became known colloquially as whalers and by 1862 that title was used officially.

Suppressing the slave trade gave rise to another variant among boats. In 1877 launches were being used for extended cruising and it was found that they were more seaworthy if built with 'pinked sterns'. It will be remembered that a pink was a type of sailing ship distinguished by her narrow, and usually high, stern. The pink-sterned launches did not last very long.

The **galley** had come into the Navy about the end of the French wars. Here again we have a number of meanings for a word. The earliest galleys were those of the Mediterranean, designed primarily to be propelled by oars, but with sails for auxiliary use when running before the wind. In the seventeenth and early eighteenth centuries there were small ships in the Royal Navy, and also some merchant vessels, which bore such names as the *Mary Galley*. These were ship-rigged and intended primarily for sailing, but they were pierced with oar-ports and supplied with oars so that they could be rowed in calms.

By the second half of the eighteenth century a type of swift boat had been evolved by smugglers and called by them a galley. In 1773 the Tide Surveyors were asking for a new boat or galley to cope with the galleys used by smugglers,[134] and thereafter the Custom House galleys, pulling six or eight oars, became common.[135] The galley supplanted the gig among boats commonly built at Deal, for in 1787 it is only mentioned among the types of boats built there.[136] The gig tended to become a south-west coast of England type.[137] As far as basic design went there could have been little to choose between them, but the galley always pulled six or eight oars, the gig usually five or less.

When they were introduced into the Royal Navy, galleys were only allowed to vessels employed in the suppression of smuggling, where light fast boats were a necessity. From about 1826 several admirals and captains asked that galleys might be allowed to certain ships for use as despatch boats,[138] but these applications were always refused until 1836, when a 33ft galley was allowed to the *Melville*, flagship on the North America and West Indies station.[139]

In the 1850s it became customary in ships of the line to allocate the first gig to the use of the captain and to call her 'the galley'. In 1860 it was approved for flag officers to have a galley as well as a barge.[140] During the next few years the old type of barge gave place to the new. No longer did the importance of a flag officer require that he should have a large double-banked boat similar to a pinnace. Instead a light fast boat better filled his needs. In 1860 we see that the barge was still a heavy diagonal-built boat.[141]

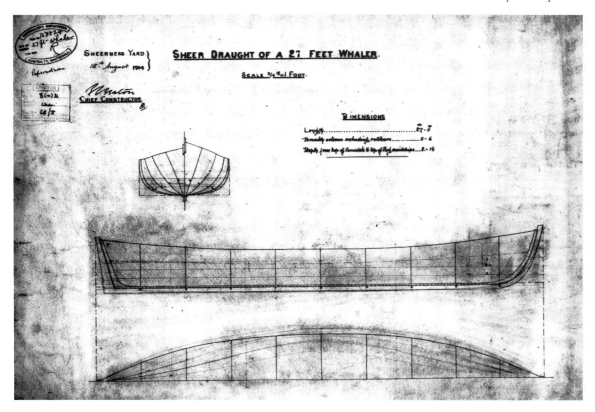

The term 'whaleboat' was soon shortened to whaler and by the end of the nineteenth century this was the official nomenclature. The lines of a 27ft whaler of 1904 are shown here. *(Bu(m)31)*

A draught of a 30ft 'life gig', dated 4 November 1873. To be effective in a life-saving role, the boat had to be fast under oars, with considerable sheer forward for seaworthiness, and to be fitted with internal air cases for added buoyancy. *(Bu(f)42a)*

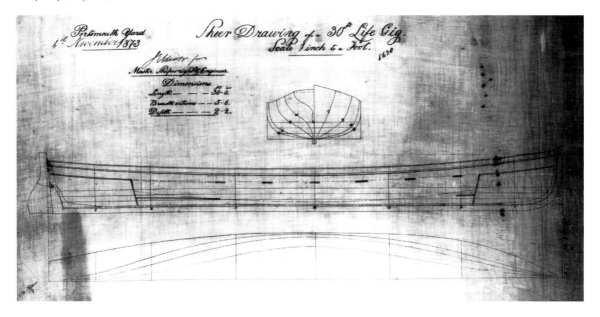

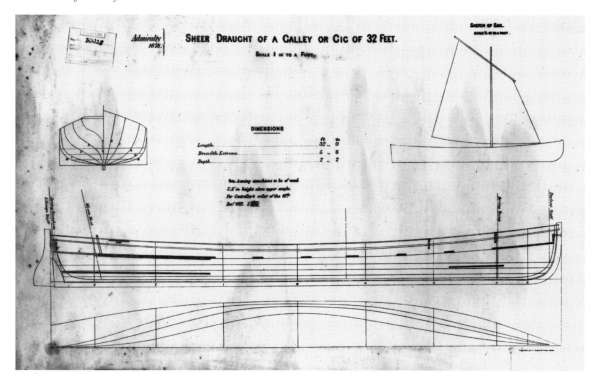

Another of the 1878 draughts, this one depicts a 32ft galley or gig. It seems to be a slightly elongated version of the 1873 life gig. (*Bu(h)2b*)

A draught of a 36ft galley of extreme proportions, designed for the new royal yacht, the *Victoria & Albert III*, 1898. (*Bu(j)48*)

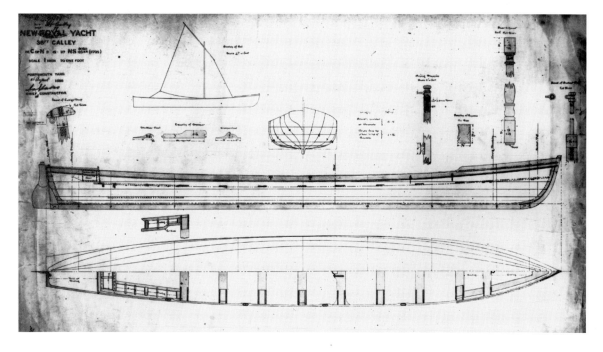

By 1877 barges were all clinker-built,[142] and these barges remained in the *Rate Book* until 1893. By this time steam barges had appeared.

From 1877 to 1886 the *Rate Book* shows gigs, galleys and whalers bracketed together as costing the same sum per foot to build. As the other two were clinker-built boats it can safely be assumed that the galleys were also clinker-built and always had been. (There is a drawing in the National Maritime Museum which shows a 32ft galley of 1867 which is apparently carvel built,[143] but I do not believe that this was the regular pattern.) From 1905 the *Rate Book* shows 32ft carvel-built single-banked galleys for the use of admirals, but they were commonly carried by ships for the use of their captains.

Paddle-box boats can be seen on this model of the steam frigate *Tiger* of 1849. (*SLR00102/B7801C*)

The introduction of paddle steamers into the Navy led to the introduction of yet another type of boat, the paddle-box boat. The peculiar form of the paddle-box suggested to Captain George Smith that it was just the place to stow a specially designed boat, bottom upwards. (Mr Barr, the Inspector of Shipwrights at Woolwich, laid claim to the invention.) These carvel-built boats appeared in 1839 and in 1844 Captain Smith was awarded the sum of £1000 for his invention.[144]

LIFEBOATS

The stranding of the *Adventure*, of Newcastle, off Tynemouth in September 1789 and the inability of any local boat to go to the rescue of her crew led in the following year to the first installation of a lifeboat to operate from our shores. This boat, designed by Mr Henry Greathead, was self-righting and being fitted with a large quantity of cork was unsinkable. A patent for another unsinkable boat had been taken out by Lionel Lukin in 1785.[145] A third type on a plan similar to Lukin's was suggested by Christopher Wilson in 1807.

The success of the shore-based lifeboats and the ease with which ships could launch their boats from the new davits no doubt led many officers to consider how the boats of their ships could be modified to improve their suitability for saving life at sea. In 1808 Greathead tried to persuade the Admiralty to establish lifeboat stations around the coast and to use boats of

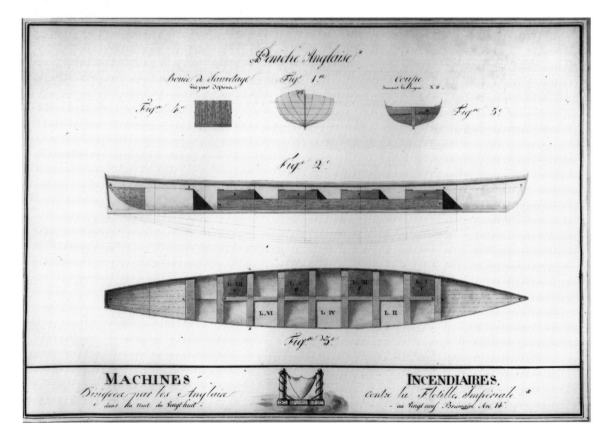

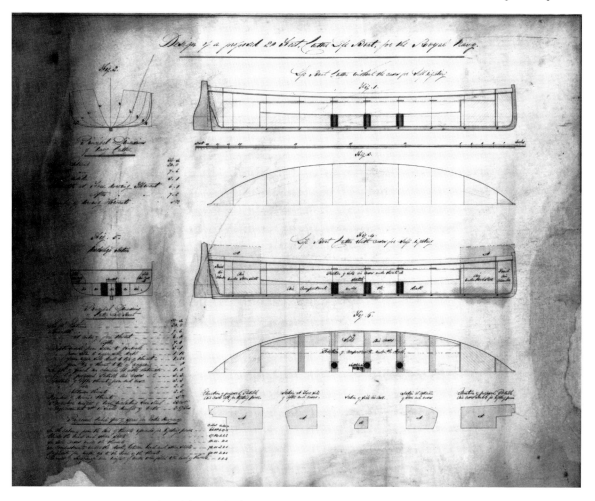

Above left Model of the patent Greathead lifeboat of about 1800. Although they were never used as warship's boats, these lifeboats were an important step in sparking naval interest in the concept of life-saving. The Admiralty planned to issue one to each of the main naval anchorages, for shore-based rescue work, but the scheme fell foul of the economists. (*2333*)

Left After the short-lived Peace of Amiens in 1802 the British Isles were seriously threatened by invasion from Napoleonic France, leading the Admiralty to adopt some of the unconventional devices of the ingenious Robert Fulton. These primitive floating mines, variously termed 'coffers' and 'infernals', were drifted down on an anchored enemy. They needed fast craft to get near enough to position them with a fair chance of hitting before being spotted, and they also needed boats to pick up the crews of the semi-submersible 'catamarans' used alongside the coffers. The result was a special gig fitted with cork buoyancy chambers to make them unsinkable, and may be regarded as the Royal Navy's first dedicated lifeboats. This French drawing is of one of the craft abandoned and captured off Boulogne. (*D9059G*)

Above A draught for a proposed (probably by the late Rear Admiral Lord John Hay) 28ft cutter lifeboat with buoyancy chambers and a temporary self-righting capability provided by 'portable air cases' fore and aft. It is undated but probably around 1860. (*Bu(b)18*)

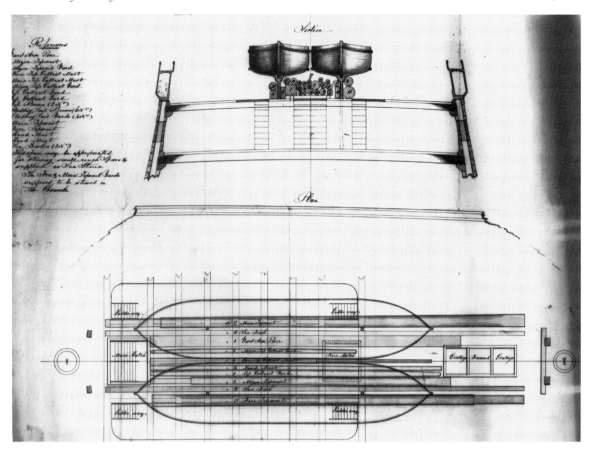

Above Instead of leaving the stowage of the boats to each ship's captain, it became
necessary to design the waist area precisely. In this plan and section of the *Indefatigable*'s
midships, dated 19 October 1848, not only the boats but the position of every spare
spar is indicated. The boats, carried above them on iron crutches, were themselves of
special design, by Lord John Hay, Chairman of the Board of Naval Construction and a
Lord of the Admiralty; they were 46ft long and double-ended. (*DR7412*)

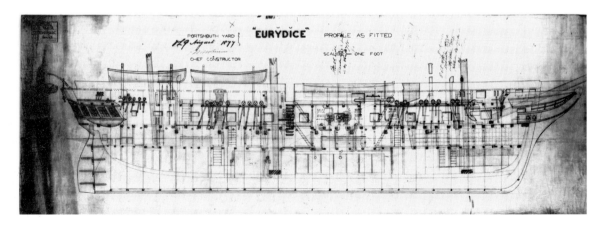

the same type in ships. The Navy Board examined his proposals and found that while it would be possible to carry lifeboats of up to 25ft in ships, owing to their shape the stowage of anything larger would not be practicable. The Board therefore suggested that a trial should be made with four or five 25ft boats in flagships, but when the Admiralty discovered that these would cost £180 each (£170 if they did not have sliding keels) compared with £11.17.0 for a jollyboat it vetoed the proposal.[146]

Another suggestion made in the same year was to build jollyboats on the self-balancing principle of Harper & Wilson, but this also was rejected. These boats would have cost £45 each, with the addition of 1/6d a foot extra if the air-gunwales were filled with cork shavings.[147] During the nineteenth century a variety of conversions of ordinary boats as lifeboats were undertaken. These mostly consisted of inserting airtight buoyancy tanks or masses of cork under the thwarts or under the gunwales. An example which lasted for some years was a 25ft, ten-oared, cork-filled cutter of special design, which was proposed in 1879 and of which a drawing has survived.[148]

HOISTING BOATS

As masts and yards disappeared it became necessary to instal a derrick in ships for lifting the larger boats out of the water. The convenience of davits led to an increase from the one or two pairs originally installed. Davits appeared all along a ship's side, but as guns came to be fitted on the centre-line instead of on the broadside, davits were swept away again to prevent their interference with arcs of fire. Ships were once more left with two pairs, usually abreast the bridge, for hoisting two boats for use as lifeboats.

An improvement which was introduced during the nineteenth century was the use of various kinds of quick–release gear for boats lowered from davits in a seaway. The dangers attendant on unhooking the forward fall first

Left below and below
Profile and upper deck plan of the *Eurydice*, as fitted in 1877. As a training ship she carried far more boats than usual: four 26ft cutters under the quarter davits; a 30ft galley at the stern; two 30ft pinnaces on the booms, with another 26ft cutter and a 14ft dinghy nested in the starboard boat.
(DR7510B & DR7512C)

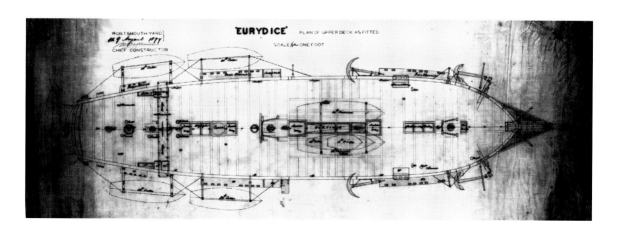

Above Boats were still stowed on deck in the last generation of sailing warships, but these were effectively flush-decked with solid waist bulwarks so required slightly different arrangements. This 1858 photograph shows a gig on the spar deck of the old frigate *Southampton* of 1820, as well as the quarter davits in the background. (*A8603Y*)

Right The introduction of turrets required the removal of many of the deck-edge davits in order to give the guns clear arcs of fire. At the same time the abandoning of masts and yards meant that a large derrick had to be installed to handle the heavier boats. These developments are clear in this view of HMS *Thunderer* of 1872, one of the first mastless modern battleships. Although seen here in 1900 after a reconstruction, the ship always had a substantial boat deck, where most of the outfit were stowed, although there are still davits for smaller boats at weather-deck level. There is a steam launch in the water, but the rest of the visible boats are traditional pulling craft. (*G5063*)

A new system of quick-release gear for the quarter-boats demonstrated in this engraving from the *Illustrated London News* for 1860. This allowed a fully manned boat to be lowered with the minimum of delay even in heavy weather. (*58/1797*)

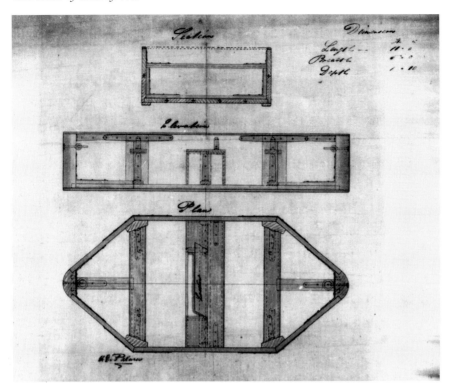

'Drawing of a Flat bottom Punt for cleaning ships copper', dated Devonport Yard 28 July 1866. (*Bu(d)8*)

if the ship had any headway are obvious. Types used in the Royal Navy with their approximate dates are as follows:

Charles Clifford[149]	1856–1881
Augustus Frederick Kynaston[150]	1858–1887
Hill & Clark	1874–1892
M H Robinson[151]	1874–1914 and later
Howard	1882–1887
Pett	1907–1914 and later

COPPERING PUNT OR BALSA RAFT

It may not be out of place here to mention a peculiar type of craft which came into use in the eighteenth century, being first mentioned in 1769.[152] This was the flat-bottomed punt for the use of artificers when they have been repairing the ship's sides or bottom. They do not appear to have had any particular form and for a long while it is doubtful whether they were actually carried to sea. A drawing of 1866[153] shows a 'Flat bottom Punt for cleaning ships copper'. It was either 11ft or 14ft long, 5 to 5½ft beam and had straight sides and triangular ends so that its plan was hexagonal. A locker was fitted in the centre. By this time the supply of punts to ships had

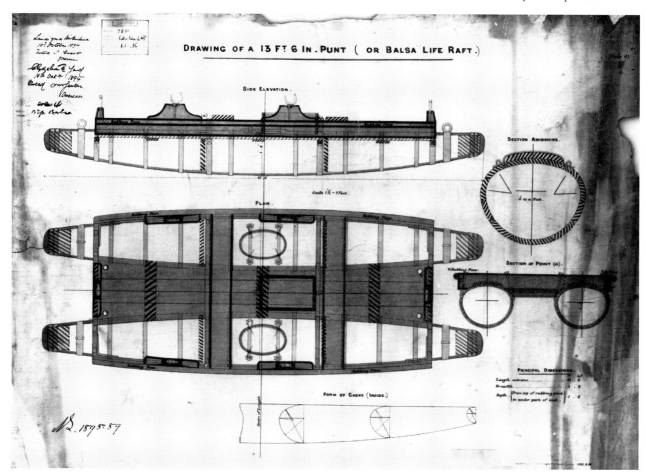

'Drawing of a 13ft 6in punt (or balsa life raft)'; annotations suggest copies were sent to Laird's, Birkenhead, and to Clydebank yard in 1894. (*DR7838*)

become usual, though it was not until 1890 that their issue to all ships which could stow them was approved.[154] By 1875 the term 'coppering punt' had come into general use and in that year Portsmouth Dockyard suggested a broad-beamed, boat-shaped type 10ft in length with a beam of 4ft 10in.[155] This was followed three years later by the adoption of a craft which was somewhat similar except that it had square ends. These came in three lengths, 14ft, 12ft and 10ft.[156] Finally in 1886 a raft arrived, formed from two elongated casks joined by a flat deck.[157] These also came in two sizes, 10ft and 14ft long. It was about this time that the abbreviated name 'copper punt' came into general use, although the official name was 'balsa raft'. In the ships built at the turn of the century which were fitted with close-stowing anchors, the copper punt was usually hoisted at the cat davit when the ship was in harbour.

Boat establishments, about 1850

	3- and 2-deckers		Rasées and frigates of 1400 tons and up		Frigates under 1400 tons		Frigates of *Vestal* class, 913 tons	
	Number-length	*Weight*	*Number-length*	*Weight*	*Number-length*	*Weight*	*Number-length*	*Weight*
Barge	1–32ft	1.17.2.2	1–32ft	1.17.2.2	1–32ft	1.17.2.2	--	--
Launch	1–40ft or 38ft	5.3.2.0	1–38ft or 36ft	4.9.2.0	1–34ft	4.1.2.0	--	--
Pinnace	1–32ft or 30ft	1.17.2.2	1–32ft or 30ft	1.17.2.2	1–30ft or 1–28ft	1.13.1.8	2–30ft	3-10-1-11
Yawl or cutter	2–26ft or 25ft	0.9.3.0	2–26ft or 25ft	0.9.3.0	1–23ft	0.8.2.0	2–23ft	0.17.0.0
Jollyboat	1–20ft	0.7.1.17	1–20ft or 18ft	0.7.1.17 0.6.2.0	1–18ft or16ft	0.6.2.0 0.5.1.14	1–16ft	0.6.2.0
Gig	1–28ft	0.7.2.0	1–28ft or 24ft	0.7.2.0 0.5.1.10	1–28ft or 24ft	0.7.2.0 0.5.1.10	1–22ft	0.5.1.10
Dinghy	--	--	--	--			1–14ft	0.4.1.0
Total	7	10.3.0.21	7	9.7.2.17	7	8.13.0.22	7	5.3.1.21

	Frigate-built sloops, 600 tons		Flush-deck ships and brigs, 18 guns		Brigs under 250 tons		Packets	
	Number-length	*Weight*	*Number-length*	*Weight*	*Number-length*	*Weight*	*Number-length*	*Weight*
Barge	--	--	--	--	--	--	--	--
Launch	--	--	--	--	--	--	1–21ft	1.0.2.0
Pinnace	1–30ft or 28ft	1.13.1.8	1–28ft or 26ft	1.10.0.22	--	--	--	--
Yawl or cutter	1–25ft or 23ft	0.8.2.0	1–23ft	0.8.2.0	1–26ft or 25ft	0.9.3.0	1–14ft	0.4.1.0
Jollyboat	1–16ft	0.5.1.14	1–16ft or 14ft	0.5.1.14 0.4.1.0	1–16ft or 14ft	0.5.1.4 0.4.1.0	1–18ft	0.6.2.0
Gig	1–24ft or 22ft	0.7.2.0 0.5.1.10	1–22ft	0.5.1.10	1–22ft	0.5.1.10	1–22ft	0.5.1.10
Dinghy	--	--	--	--	--	--	--	--
Total	4	2.13.2.13	4	2.8.3.11	3	0.19.3.17	4	1.16.0.10

Weight is given in tons.cwt.qrs.lbs.
Schooner and cutters carried one 11ft yawl/cutter and one 11ft jollyboat, each weighing 3cwt.
From John Scott Russell, *The Modern System of Naval Architecture* (London 1865).

The principal dimensions, average weights, life-saving capacity, etc, of boats used in Her Majesty's service, 1886

Description of Boat	Dimensions of Boats			Number of Oars, &c.					Weight of Boat, &c.				Will carry men in moderate weather
	Length	Breadth	Depth	Oars all manned	Oars spare	Length	Number	Total Number	Boat	Mast Gear	Oars	Slings	
	ft in	ft in	ft in			ft in			T C qrs lbs	C qrs lbs	C qrs lbs	C qrs lbs	
Launch	42 0	11 0	4 3	18	2	17 0 / 16 0	16 / 4	20	4 10 0 0	4 2 23	1 2 21	3 2 16	140
	40 0	10 8	4 0	16	2	17 0 / 16 0	14 / 4	18	4 3 3 10	4 0 0 0	1 2 2	3 0 0	127
	38 0	10 4	3 9	16	2	17 0 / 16 0	14 / 4	18	3 18 1 20	3 2 10	1 2 2	3 0 0	109
	36 0	9 8	3 4	16	2	17 0 / 16 0	14 / 4	18	3 14 3 10	3 1 6	1 2 2	2 3 0	86
Pinnace	32 0	9 0	3 3	14	2	16 0 / 15 0	12 / 4	16	2 8 0 2	2 2 10	1 1 9	2 1 0	70
	30 0	8 9	3 2	12	2	16 0 / 15 0	10 / 4	14	2 5 0 0	2 0 25	1 0 14	2 0 0	62
	28 0	8 6	3 0	12	2	16 0 / 15 0	10 / 4	14	2 2 0 0	1 3 13	1 0 14	1 3 0	53
	26 0	8 6	2 11	12	2	15 0 / 14 0	10 / 4	14	1 17 0 0	1 3 6	1 0 14	1 2 0	48
Cutter	34 0	8 10	2 11½	12	2	15 0 / 14 0	10 / 4	14	1 2 0 0	1 2 7	1 0 14	1 2 16	66
	32 0	8 6	2 11	12	2	15 0 / 14 0	10 / 4	14	19 3 0	1 2 7	1 0 14	1 2 0	59
	30 0	8 1	2 8½	12	2	15 0 / 14 0	10 / 4	14	18 1 0	1 2 7	1 0 14	1 2 0	49
	28 0	7 6	2 6½	10	2	15 0 / 14 0	8 / 4	12	17 0 0	1 2 7	0 3 21	1 1 0	40
	26 0	7 4½	2 6	8	2	14 0 / 13 0	6 / 4	10	16 1 14	1 1 10	0 3 0	1 1 0	36
	25 0	7 3	2 5½	8	2	14 0 / 13 0	6 / 4	10	15 0 0	1 0 27	0 3 0	1 1 0	34
	23 0	6 11	2 4½	8	2	14 0 / 13 0	6 / 4	10	13 0 0	1 0 10	0 3 0	1 0 22	27
	20 0	6 4	2 3	8	2	14 0 / 13 0	6 / 4	10	10 0 8	0 3 10	0 3 0	1 0 0	21
	18 0	6 0	2 2	6	2	14 0 / 13 0	4 / 4	8	8 3 0	0 3 0	0 2 11	0 3 0	17
	16 0	5 7	2 1	6	2	14 0 / 13 0	4 / 4	8	7 1 10	0 2 18	0 2 11	0 2 19	14
Dingy	14 0	5 2	2 2	4	nil	12 6	4	4	4 3 0	0 0 21	0 1 4		10
	12 0	5 0	2 1	4	nil	11 0	4	4	3 3 0	0 0 18	0 1 0		9
Admiral's Barge	34 0	7 10	2 9	14	2	15 0 / 14 0	12 / 4	16	1 30 0	1 2 7	1 0 14	1 2 16	54
Galley	32 0	5 6	2 2	6	1	17 0 / 16 0	5 / 2	7	9 2 0	0 1 18	0 2 7		28
Gig	32 0	5 6	2 2	6	1	17 0 / 16 0	5 / 2	7	9 1 0	0 1 18	0 2 7		28
	30 0	5 6	2 2	6	1	17 0 / 16 0	5 / 2	7	9 0 0	0 1 18	0 2 7		26
	28 0	5 6	2 2	6	1	17 0 / 16 0	5 / 2	7	8 1 14	0 1 18	0 2 7		25
	27 0	5 6	2 2	5	1	17 0 / 16 0	4 / 2	6	8 0 0	0 1 16	0 1 26		24

Description of Boat	Dimensions of Boats — Length	Breadth	Depth	Number of Oars — Oars all manned	Oars spare	Length	Number	Total Number	Weight of Boat — Boat (T C qrs lbs)	Mast Gear (C qrs lbs)	Oars (C qrs lbs)	Slings (C qrs lbs)	Will carry men in moderate weather
	ft in	ft in	ft in			ft in			T C qrs lbs	C qrs lbs	C qrs lbs	C qrs lbs	
	26 0	5 6	2 2	5	1	17 0	4	6	7 3 0	0 1 15	0 1 26		23
						16 0	2						
	25 0	5 6	2 2	5	1	17 0	4	6	7 1 14	0 1 14	0 1 26		22
						16 0	2						
	24 0	5 6	2 2	4	1	16 0	3	5	7 0 0	0 1 13	0 1 14		21
						15 0	2						
	23 0	5 6	2 2	4	1	16 0	3	5	6 3 14	0 1 0	0 1 14		20
						15 0	2						
	22	5 6	2 2	4	1	16 0	3	5	6 3 0	0 1 6	0 1 14		19
						15 0	2						
	20	5 6	2 2	4	1	15 0	3	5	5 3 0	0 1 2	0 1 14		18
						14 0	2						
Cutter Gig	20	5 6	2 2	4	1	15 0	3	5	6 0 0	0 1 2	0 1 14		18
						14 0	2						
Life Gigs Whale or otherwise	32	5 6	2 2½	6	1	15 0	5	7	13 0 0	0 1 18	0 2 7		28
						14 0	2						
	30	5 6	2 2	6	1	15 0	5	7	11 3 0	0 1 18	0 2 7		26
						14 0	2						
	28	5 6	2 2	6	1	15 0	5	7	10 3 14	0 1 18	0 2 7		25
						14 0	2						
	27	5 6	2 2	5	1	15 0	4	6	9 2 14	0 1 16	0 1 24		24
						14 0	2						
	25	5 6	2 2	5	1	15 0	4	6	9 3 21	0 1 14	0 1 24		22
						14 0	2						
	24	5 6	2 2	4	1	15 0	3	5	8 2 0	0 1 13	0 1 14		21
						14 0	2						
	23	5 6	2 2	4	1	15 0	3	5	8 0 16	0 1 12	0 1 14		20
						14 0	2						
Troop Boat	38	8 6	3 2	16	2	15 0	14	18	1 5 0 0	1 2 7	1 1 22	1 2 24	80
						14 0	4						
Troop life	38	8 6	3 2	16	2	15 0	14	18	1 6 0 0	1 2 7	1 1 22	1 2 24	80
						14 0	4						
Cutter Life	32	8 11	3 1	10	2	15 0	8	12	1 10 0 0	1 1 0	0 3 21	1 3 14	70
						14 0	4						
	30	8 3	3 1	10	2	15 0	8	12	1 6 0 0	1 0 20	0 3 21	1 3 0	60
						14 0	4						
	28	7 6	3 1	10	2	14 0	8	12	1 0 0 0	1 0 10	0 3 0	1 2 14	50
						13 0	4						
	25	7 6	2 10	8	2	14 0	6	10	16 2 0	1 0 0	0 3 0	1 1 0	40
						13 0	4						
Steam Launch	42	11 0	4 3	18	2	17 0	16	20	5 12 0 0	4 2 23	1 2 21	3 2 16	70
						16 0	4						
Steam Pinnace	37	8 11	4 7½	4	nil	14 0	2	4	6 2 0 0	1 2 24	0 1 5		50
						13 0	2						
	30	7 7	4 2	4	nil	14 0	2	4	4 15 0 0	0 2 25	0 1 5		38
						13 0	2						
Cutter	28	7 3	3 9½	4	nil	14 0	2	4	3 4 0 0	0 2 9	0 1 5		32
						13 0	2						
	25	6 3	3 4	4	nil	14 0	2	4	2 10 0 0	0 1 14	0 1 5		24
						13 0	2						
	22	6 0	2 11	4	nil	14 0	2	4	2 0 0 0	0 1 10	0 1 5		20
						13 0	2						

Weights are tons, hundredweight, quarters and pounds.

From Sir George Nares, *Practical Seamanship*, 1886 edition.

Table of boats' weights, etc, 1908

Boat	Length	Weight	Sail Area	Length of Grapnel	Size of Grapnel	Weight of Anchor	Life-saving Capacity	Length of Mast	Diam of Mast	Length of Gaff	Diam of Gaff	Remarks
	Feet	Tons cwt	Sq ft	Fathoms	Chain	Lbs		Ft Ins	Ins	Ft Ins	Ins	
Steam pinnaces	56	18 0		40	3/8"	120	80					The weights of the steam boats are inclusive of water in tanks and in boiler to working height, half coal and provisions, but no armament or men
	45	12 0		40	3/8"	120	60					
	40	12 8		40	3/8"	100	50					
Steam cutters	32	5 15		40	5/16"	50	40					
	23	3 0		25	1/4"	30	21					
Steam barges	40	10 11		40	3/8"	100	50					
	32	5 3		40	5/16"	50	40					
Launch	42	7 17	754	40	3/8"	120	140	36 7	7	19 0	4¼	The weights of the pulling boats are exclusive of countermining gear, gear for laying out anchors, men and armament, but includes all other gear
Pinnaces	36	5 0	566	40	3/8"	90	86	32 0	6	17 6	3½	
	32	4 12	418	40	5/16"	70	70	28 0	6	15 9	3½	
	30	3 13	368	40	5/16"	60	62	26 11	5I	14 6	3¼	

Boat	Length	Weight	Sail Area	Length of Grapnel	Size of Grapnel	Weight of Anchor	Life-saving Capacity	Masts Main		Fore		Yards Main		Fore	
	Feet	Tons cwt	Sq ft	Fathoms	Hemp	Lbs		Length Ft Ins	Diam Ins	Length Ft Ins	Diam Ins	Length Ft Ins	Ins	Diam Ft Ins	Ins
Cutter	34	2 3	449	30	3½"	40	66	20 10	4½	23 2	4¾	12 4	3	14 3	3⅛
	32	2 0	382	30	3½"	40	59	20 2	4¾	22 0	4¾	11 6	3	13 6	3
	30	1 18	357	30	3½"	40	49	19 6	4½	21 0	4¾	11 0	3	13 0	3
	28	1 13	324	30	3½"	40	40	19 3	4½	20 3	4¾	10 3	3	12 9	3
	26	1 8	321	30	3½"	40	36	14 6★	3½★	22 0	4½	10 9★	2½★	12 2	3
Galley	32	0 17	251	25	3"	30	28	13 6	3½	12 4	3½	19 6	2½	15 9	2½
Gig	30	0 16	224	25	3"	30	26	12 10	3½	11 7	3½	19 0	2½	15 6	2⅜
	28	0 15	189	25	3"	30	25	12 4	3½	11 4	3½	17 6	2½	13 10	2⅝
Whaler	27	0 14	168	25	3"	30	24	12 4	3½	11 4	3½	17 0	2½	13 9	2⅝
Dinghy	13½	0 6	71	20	2½"	20	9								
Skiff Dinghy	16	0 5.5	75	20	2½"	20	10	12 0	2½			Sprit			
Punt	13½	0 8		20	2½"	20	8					11 6	1⅝		
	10	0 5					6								

★ Mizen

From the *Admiralty Manual of Seamanship*, 1908 edition.

A draught of the masting and rigging of a 32ft longboat, undated but mid–eighteenth century. *(Bu(h)12)*

Chapter 4   SAILS AND RIGGING

We have seen that the early boats had but a single sail, but by the eighteenth century this was no longer true. In 1713 an inventory of stores in the *Litchfield* (48 guns), gives two sails for her 32ft pinnace and three for her yawl.[158] In 1750 Blanckley illustrated a longboat with a gaff-headed, loose-footed mainsail, a triangular foresail and a jib rigged to a bowsprit.[159]

In 1761 the cutters of 21ft upwards which were built at Deal had two masts and two sails with sprits. The 18ft cutters had a single mast and sprit-sail.[160] In this year it was reported that captains were re-rigging their cutters with a main and mizen mast, and Deal was ordered to fit this rig in any future cutters that they might build.[161]

When gigs were introduced into the service in 1763 they were rigged with a lug mainsail and a mizen. In 1763 an order to the yards gave directions as to the proper lengths for boat spars.[162] These enable us to get a good idea of how each type of boat was rigged. The longboat was still rigged as in 1750, except that the mainsail now had a boom. In a 74-gun ship, whose boat had a 10ft beam, the mast was 30ft long, the bowsprit 15ft, the boom 23ft 4in and the gaff 9ft 9in.

The barge, pinnace and yawl were rigged alike with two masts carrying sprit sails of equal size. The barge of a 74-gun ship had a beam of 6ft 6in, had 16ft masts and 18ft 'spreets', dimensions for the other boats being in proportion.

The cutters had main and mizen masts, the main sail having a yard and the mizen a sprit, rigged to an outrigger. We see here the result of the instruction of 1761 quoted above. The larger of the two cutters of a 74 had a beam of 7ft 4in, masts 20ft 2in and 12ft 7in, with a yard 10ft 1in, a sprit 14ft 2in, and an outrigger 8ft 5in. Drawings show that the pinnace usually had her masts at about one tenth and one half of her length from the bow. It appears that some officers at this date were rigging their boats as schooners instead of ketches.

In 1803 a new rig with a mizen appeared for the launch,[163] which had been rigged the same as a longboat. By 1857 all launches, pinnaces and barges were ketch rigged, with a foresail and bowsprit, a mainsail with yard and a large mizen with yard and boom.[164] In 1860 Rear-Admiral Sir Charles Elliot and Captain Richard Strode Hewlett proposed the adoption of schooner rigs for launches, pinnaces and barges. It was tried out in 1861 in a number of boats of the last two types. It was found that there was little if

Above With the exception of early barges and pinnaces, ship's boats were not optimised for rowing, so boat crews took every opportunity to carry sail. In Dominic Serres' magnificent panoramic painting of the British fleet entering Havana on 21 August 1762, most of the ships – including Admiral Pocock's flagship, the 90-gun *Namur* in the foreground – are shown towing their largest boat. However, a longboat accompanies the fleet under the usual cutter rig, while a smaller boat is also under sail, carrying a single sprit sail. (*BHC0415*)

any advantage to be gained from the sailing and handling points of view, but the foremast needed to be moved slightly and this did not allow sufficient room for the carronade to be worked. In addition the bowsprit did not permit the carronade to be trained fore-and-aft and if it were trained on the beam it gave the boat a list, which upset her sailing qualities. The Admiralty ordered that the dipping lug rig should be retained in the barge and pinnace, and that further trials should be made in the launch.[165] This led in 1865 to a fresh proposal from Admiral Elliot, for a sketch exists of a 40ft launch with a schooner rig, having two masts stepped at approximately a quarter and just over half the length of the boat from the bow, and a bowsprit. This rig was evidently adopted for it also appears in a drawing of 1878.

Right A contemporary model of the *Medway*'s 28ft longboat with its cutter rig, with the bowsprit rigged through an iron ring on the starboard side of the stemhead. The mainsail has a boom, suggesting that Blanckley's illustration of a loose-footed sail, published in 1750, actually reflects earlier practice. Note also the presence of runner backstays. (*SLR0330/D5407*)

Below Official drawings of boat sails, dated Devonport Yard 15 July 1869. The top row
are cutters – 28ft, 25ft (in pencil '26 feet'), 23ft; second row, three lengths of jollyboat
(20ft, 18ft, 16ft) and 14ft and 12ft dinghies; third row, gigs – 30ft (in pencil '33 feet'),
28ft (in pencil '28ft, 27ft'), 24ft and 22ft; bottom row, 20ft cutter gig, 27ft whaleboat,
and 25ft whaleboat. (*Bu(g)6f&6g*)

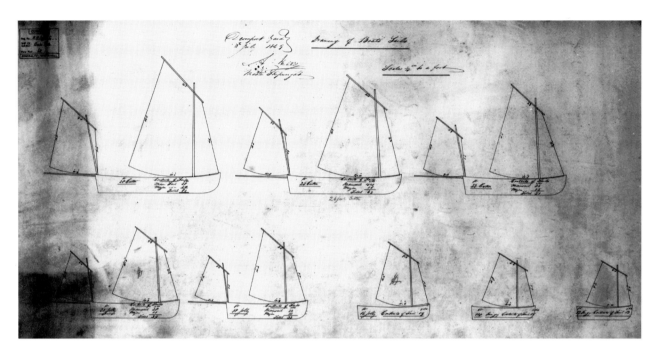

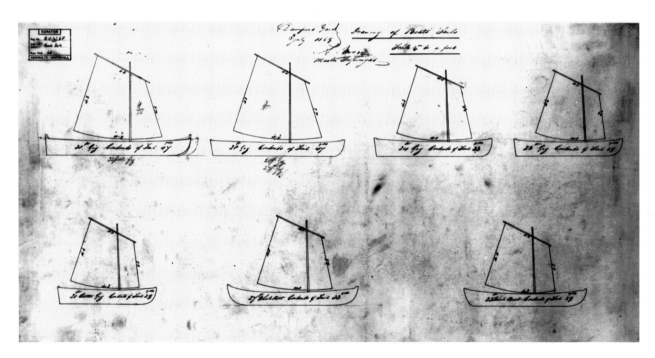

A drawing of the
original de Horsey rig,
dated Chatham Yard
October 1884.
(*Bu(e)28*)

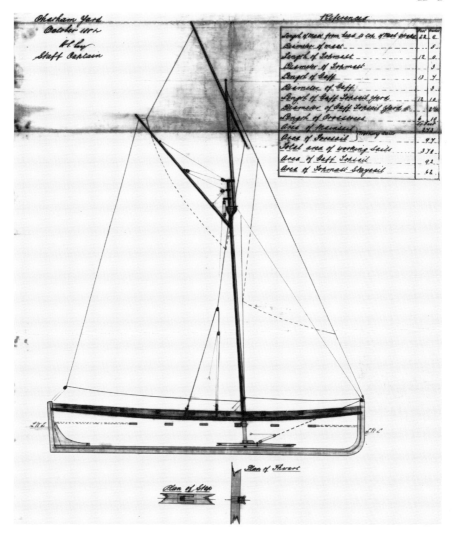

The officially
sanctioned version of
the de Horsey rig,
without topmast, as
seen in the 1908
edition of the
*Admiralty Manual of
Seamanship.* (*E0360*)

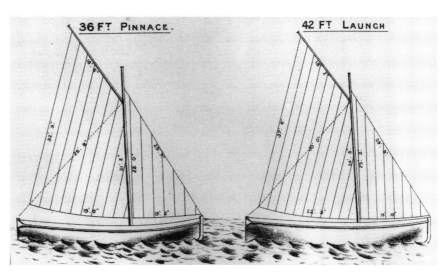

In 1884 Vice-Admiral Algernon Frederick Roos de Horsey proposed a single-masted rig without a bowsprit, having a gaff-headed, loose-footed mainsail and triangular foresail, to which could be added a topmast, topsail and topmast-staysail. The de Horsey rig was adopted for launches, pinnaces and for some cutters, but without the topmast and its two associated sails. Some officers fitted these at their own expense.

A series of drawings made in 1869 shows the rigs of some boats then in vogue, and these do not appear to have changed much in the previous century. Cutters of 28ft, 25ft and 23ft and jollyboats of 20ft and 18ft had a dipping-lug mainsail and a standing-lug mizen, while 16ft jollyboats, 14ft and 12ft dinghies, 28ft, 24ft, 22ft and 20ft gigs and 2ft and 25ft whaleboats had a single mast and dipping lug-sail. In 1882 there was a proposal to replace this single dipping lug-sail of the whaler by a two-masted rig, consisting of a foresail, triangular mainsail and small triangular mizen, but whalers, together with galleys and gigs were given two equal masts, each with a dipping lug-sail. It was not until the early years of the present century that the Montagu whaler appeared. This boat, partially following the proposals of Rear-Admiral Victor Alexander Montagu, had a fuller body aft and was

Even the new steam boats were fitted to carry sail when required. This draught shows the sails for a 45ft steam pinnace, dated 6 November 1879. *(BS(e)14)*

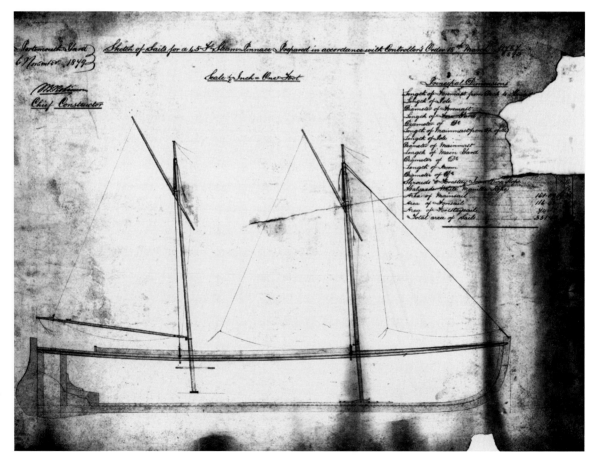

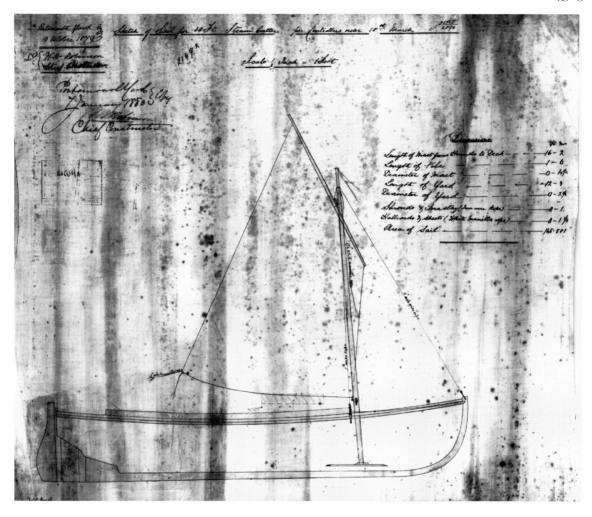

Above A draught of the rig for a 30ft steam cutter, dated 10 October 1879. *(BS(b)19e)*

Below A mid-nineteenth century single-masted dipping-lug rig for a 30ft gig, as represented in the 1882 edition of *Nares' Manual of Seamanship*. *(E0358)*

Below right A 27ft whaler with two dipping-lug sails as fitted from the 1880s; from the 1908 edition of the *Admiralty Manual of Seamanship*. *(E0359)*

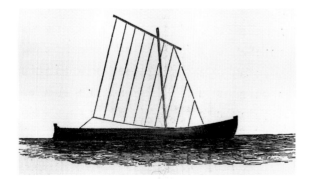

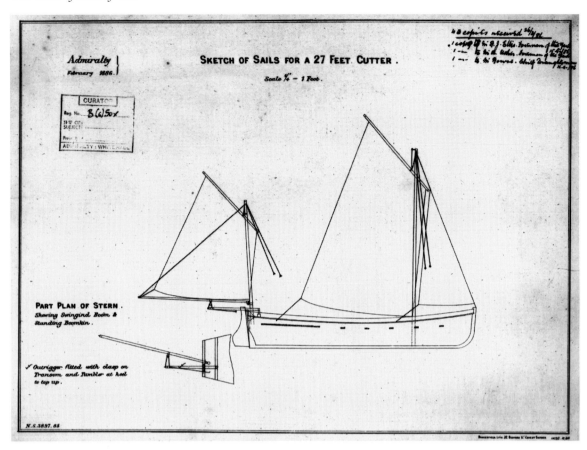

A draught of February 1886 showing the altered rig for a 27ft cutter, with a
dipping-lug foresail and a standing-lug mizen. (*Bu(g)50X*)

The dimensions of rigging, with the species, sizes and number of blocks, etc, 1794

Names of the standing and running rigging	110 to 74 guns In	Blocks, &c Species	In	No	64 guns In	Blocks, &c Species	In	No	50 to 36 guns In	Blocks, &c Species	In	No
Longboat's rigging												
Burton pendents	4	S.	11	2	4	S.	11	2	3½	S.	9	2
Runner	3	T.		2	3	T.		2	2½	T.		2
Falls	{ 2½	*D.	9	2	2½	*D.	9	2	2	*D.	9	2
	{ 2½	*S.	9	2	2½	*S.	9	2	2	*S.	9	2
Strapping	3				3				2½			2
Shrouds	4	D.E.	5	4	3½	D.E.	5	4	3	T.		4
Laniard	1½				1½				1			
Stay	4½	D.E.	5	1	4	D.E.	5	1	3½	T.		1
Laniard	1½				1½				1			
Tie	3	S.	9	1	3	S.	9	1	3	S.	9	1
Main haliard	2	S.	7	2	2	S.	7	2	1½	S.	6	1
Outer haliard	{ 2	D.I.bd.	7	1	2	D.I.bd.	7	1	1½	D.I.bd.	6	1
	{ 2	*S.	7	1	2	*S.	7	1	1½	*S.	6	1

The cutter from the armoured cruiser *King Alfred* being sailed at Wei-Hai-Wei, China about 1906. A rear-admiral's flag is carried as a crest forward, by this date a common practice in flagships. (*N11556*)

rigged with a standing-lug mainsail, triangular foresail and small triangular mizen.

In 1883 proposals were made for altering the rig of cutters and it was about this time that the rig for the larger boats, above 26ft, was altered to a dipping-lug foresail and standing-lug mizen.

About 1868 Vice-Admiral Sir Henry Keppel, who was then Commander-in-Chief in China, had his flag painted on the bows of the boats of the *Rodney*. The Admiralty heard of it and objected, ordering him to have them removed.[166] During the next decade the practice of carrying a ship's crest on the bows of her boats became fashionable, a photograph of the *Lord Warden* taken about 1870 showing this. Another photograph, taken about 1880, shows the boats of the *Agincourt* displaying on their bows the flag of the rear-admiral, second in command of the Channel Squadron.

32 to 28 guns				24 guns				22 to 20 guns				18 to 14 guns			
In	Blocks, &c			In	Blocks, &c			In	Blocks, &c			In	Blocks, &c		
	Species	In	No		Species	In	No		Species	In	No		Species	In	No
3½	S.	9	2	3	S.	8	2	3	S.	8	2				
2½	T.		2	2½	T.		2	2½	T.		2				
2	★D.	8	2	2	★D.	8	2	2	★D.	8	2				
2	★S.	8	2	2	★S.	8	2	2	★S.	8	2				
2½				2½				2½							
3	T.		4	3	T.		4	3	T.		4				
I				I				I							
3½	T.		I	3½	T.		I	3½	T.		I	2			
I				I				I							
1½	S.	6	I	1½	S.	6	I	I	S.	5	I	I			
1½	D.I.bd.	6	I	1½	D.I.bd.	6	I	I	D.I.bd.	5	I				
1½	★S.	6	I	1½	★S.	6	I	I	★S.	5	I				

Names of the standing and running rigging	110 to 74 guns				64 guns				50 to 36 guns			
	In	Blocks, &c Species	In	No	In	Blocks, &c Species	In	No	In	Blocks, &c Species	In	No
Longboat's rigging												
Sheet	{ 2	D.	8	1	2	D.	8	1	1½	S.	6	2
	{ 2	★S.	8	1	2	★S.	8	1	1½	T.		1
Wooden hoops												
Downhauler	1½	S.	5	1	1½	S.	5	1	1	S.	5	1
Strapping	2				2				1½			
Topping lifts	2½				2				1½			
Fore haliard	2	S.	7	1	2	S.	7	1	2	S.	7	1
Sheet	2	T.		2	2	T.		2	2	T.		2
Tack	1				1				1			
Bowline	2½	T.		1	2½	T.		1	2			
Jib haliard	{ 2	S.	7	2	2	S.	7	2	2	S.	7	1
	{ 2	★		1	2	★		1	2	S.	7	1
Sheet	2½	T.		4	2½				2			
Out-hauler	3	I. Tra.		1	2½	I. Tra.		1	2	I. Tra.		1
In-hauler	1				1				1			
Boat-rope cabled	9				7½				6½			
Laniard	2½				2½				2			
Guest-rope cabled	5				4				3			
Grapnel-rope cabled	4½	T.		1	4				3½	T.		1
Painter	4	T.		1	4	T.		1	3½	T.		1
Sternfast	3½	T.		1	3½	T.		1	3	T.		1
Fenders cabled	6				6	T.		1	5			
Laniards	2				2				1½			
Rudder laniards	2				2				1½			
Pinnace's rigging												
Haliards, main	1½				1½				1½			
Haliards, fore	1½				1½				1½			
Sheets	1½				1½				1½			
Grapnel-rope cabled	3½	T.		1	3½			1	3½	T.		1
Painter	3½	T.		1	3½	T.		1	3½	T.		1
Sternfast	2½	T.		1	2½	T.		1	2	T.		1
Slings	5½	H.&T.	8	12	5½	H.&T.	8	12	5	H.&T.	4	6
Seizings	1				1				¾			
Rudder laniards	1				1				1			
Yawl, Cutter or Pinnace												
Main and fore haliards (if cutters)	2	I. Tra.		2	2	I. Tra.		2	1	I. Tra.		2
Main sheets	2½				2				2			
Fore sheets	2½				1½				1½			1½
Grapnel-rope cabled	3½	T.		1	3½	T.		1	3½	T.		1
Painter	3½	T.		1	3½	T.		1	3½	T.		1
Sternfast												
Slings	5½	H.&T.	8	12	5½	H.&T.	8	12	5½	H.&T.	8	12
Seizings	1				1				1			
Rudder laniards	1				1				1			

Key to abbreviations:

S = single; D = double; T = thimble; D.E. = deadeye; I. bd. = iron bound; I.Tra. = iron traveller;
H.&T. = heart and thimble; ★ = with a hook and thimble

32 to 28 guns				24 guns				22 to 20 guns				18 to 14 guns			
In	Blocks, &c Species	In	In	No	Blocks, &c Species	In	No	In	Blocks, &c Species	In	No	In	Blocks, &c Species	In	No
1½	S.	6	2	1½	S.	6	2	1	S.	5	2	1			
1½	T.		1	1½	T.		1	1	T.		1				
1	S.	5	1					1							
1½								1							
1½								1							
2	S.	7	1					1				1			
2	T.		2	1½	T.		2	1				1			
1				1				1							
2				1½				1							
2	S.	7	1	1½				1							
2	S.	7	1	1½				1							
2				1½				1				1			
2	I.Tra.		1	1½	I.Tra.		1	1	I.Tra.		1	1			
1				¾				¾							
6				4½				4½							
2				2				2							
3				3				3							
3½	T.		1	3½	T.		1	3½	T.		1	3	T.		1
3½	T.		1	3½	T.		1	3	T.		1	3	T.		1
3	T.		1	2	T.		1	2	T.		1	3			
4				4				3½				3			
1½				1½				1				1			
1½				1				1				1			
1½				1½				1½							
1½				1½				1½							
1½				1½				1½							
3½	T.		1	3½	T.		1	3½	T.		1				
3½	T.		1	3½	T.		1	3½	T.		1				
2	T.		1	2	T.		1	2	T.		1				
5	H.&T.	4	6	5	H.&T.	4	6	5	H.&T.	4	6				
1				1				1							
1				1				1							
1	I.Tra.		2	1				1				1½			
2				2				2				1½			
			1½				1				1½				
3½	T.		6	3½	T.		1	3½	T.		1	3½	T.		1
3½	T.		6	3½	T.		1	3½	T.		1	3½	T.		1
												2	T.		1
5½	H.&T.	4	6	5½	H.&T.	4	6	5½	H.&T.	4	6	4½	H.&T.	4	6
1				1				1				1			
1				1				1				1			

From David Steel, *The Elements and Practice of Rigging and Seamanship* (London 1794).

Boats: diameters of masts, booms, etc, 1854

	Of masts						Of booms gaffs, yards, bowsprits, outriggers, and slides, or topmasts, to sliding-gunter masts and sprits														
							Schooner rigged			Lugger						Sliding gunter			Lateen rigged		
Length of masts	Schooner rigged	Lugger rigged	Spirit-sail rigged	Sliding-gunter rigged	Lateen rigged	Mizen mast	Boom	Gaff	Bowsprit	Yards	Bowsprit.	Outrigger	Bowsprit	Outrigger	Sprits	Boomkin	Outrigger	Slides	Boomkin	Outrigger	Yards
one inch to feet	4.5 ins	4.4 ins	4.4 ins	4 ins	3.6 ins	3.4 ins	5.5 ins	3.2 ins	2.5 ins	5 ins	2.5 ins	3 ins	2.5 ins	3 ins	9 ins	2.5 ins	3 ins	5.4 ins	2.4 ins	3 ins	5 ins
43	9 ½	9 ¾	9 ¾	10 ¾	12										4 ¾	12					8 ⅝
42	9 ⅜	9 ½	9 ½	10 ½	11 ⅝										4 ⅝	11 ⅝					8 ⅜
41	9 ⅛	9 ⅜	9 ⅜	10 ¼	11 ⅜										4 ½	11 ¼					8 ¼
40	8 ⅞	9	9	10	11 ⅛										4 ½	10 ¾					8
39	8 ⅝	8 ⅞	8 ⅞	9 ¾	10 ⅞										4 ⅜	10 ⅜					7 ¾
38	8 ½	8 ⅝	8 ⅝	9 ½	10 ½										4 ¼						7 ⅝
37	8 ¼	8 ⅜	8 ⅜	9 ¼	10 ½										4 ⅛						7 ⅜
36	8	8 ⅛	8 ⅛	9	10 ¼										4						7 ¼
35	7 ¾	8	8	8 ¾	9 ¾										3 ⅞						7
34	7 ½	7 ¾	7 ¾	8 ½	9 ½										3 ¾						6 ¾
33	7 ⅜	7 ½	7 ½	8 ¼	9 ⅛										3 ⅝						6 ⅝
32	7 ⅛	7 ¼	7 ¼	8	8 ⅞										3 ½						6 ⅜
31	6 ⅞	7	7	7 ¾	8 ⅝										3 ½						6 ¼
30	6 ⅜	6 ⅞	6 ⅞	7 ½	8 ⅜	8 ⅞	5 ½	9 ⅜	12	6	12	10	12	10	3 ⅜	12	10	5 ½	12 ½	10	6
29	6 ⅜	6 ⅝	6 ⅝	7 ¼	8	8 ½	5 ¼	9	11 ⅝	5 ¾	11 ⅝	9 ⅝	11 ⅝	9 ⅝	3 ¼	11 ⅝	9 ⅝	5 ⅝	12 ⅛	9 ⅝	5 ¾
28	6 ¼	6 ⅜	6 ⅜	7	7 ¾	8 ¼	5 ⅛	8 ¾	11 ¼	5 ⅝	11 ¼	9 ⅜	11 ¼	9 ⅜	3 ⅛	11 ¼	9 ⅜	5 ⅛	11 ⅝	9 ⅜	5 ⅝
27	6	6 ⅛	6 ⅛	6 ¾	7 ½	8	4 ⅞	8 ⅜	10 ¾	5 ⅜	10 ¾	9	10 ¾	9	3	10 ¾	9	5	11 ¼	9	5 ⅜
26	5 ¾	5 ⅞	5 ⅞	6 ½	7 ¼	7 ⅝	4 ¾	8 ⅛	10 ⅜	5 ¼	10 ⅜	8 ⅝	10 ⅜	8 ⅝	2 ⅞	10 ⅜	8 ⅝	4 ⅞	10 ⅝	8 ⅝	5 ¼
25	5 ½	5 ⅝	5 ⅝	6 ¼	7	7 ⅜	4 ½	7 ¾	10	5	10	8 ⅜	10	8 ⅜	2 ¾	10	8 ⅜	4 ⅝	10 ⅜	8 ⅜	5
24	5 ⅜	5 ½	5 ½	6	6 ⅝	7	4 ⅜	7 ½	9 ⅝	4 ¾	9 ⅝	8	9 ⅝	8	2 ⅝	9 ⅝	8	4 ½	10	8	4 ¾
23	5 ⅛	5 ¼	5 ¼	5 ¾	6 ⅜	6 ¾	4 ⅛	7 ⅛	9 ¼	4 ⅞	9 ¼	7 ⅝	9 ¼	7 ⅝	2 ½	9 ¼	7 ⅝	4 ¼	9 ⅝	7 ⅝	4 ⅝
22	5	5	5	5 ½	6 ⅛	6 ½	4	6 ⅞	8 ¾	4 ⅜	8 ¾	7 ⅜	8 ¾	7 ⅜	2 ½	8 ¾	7 ⅜	4 ⅛	9 ⅛	7 ⅜	4 ⅜
21	4 ⅞	4 ⅞	4 ⅞	5 ¼	5 ⅞	6 ⅛	3 ⅞	6 ½	8 ⅜	4 ¼	8 ⅜	7	8 ⅜	7	2 ⅜	8 ⅜	7	3 ⅞	8 ¾	7	4 ¼
20	4 ¾	4 ¾	4 ¾	5	5 ½	5 ⅞	3 ⅝	6 ¼	8	4	8	6 ⅝	8	6 ⅝	2 ¼	8	6 ⅝	3 ¾	8 ⅜	6 ⅝	4
19	4 ⅝	4 ⅝	4 ⅝	4 ¾	5 ¼	5 ⅝	3 ⅜	5 ⅞	7 ⅝	3 ¾	7 ⅝	6 ⅜	7 ⅝	6 ⅜	2 ⅛	7 ⅝	6 ⅜	3 ½	7 ⅞	6 ⅜	3 ⅞
18	4 ½	4 ½	4 ½	4 ½	5	5 ¼	3 ½	5 ⅝	7 ¼	3 ⅝	7 ¼	6	7 ¼	6	2	7 ¼	6	3 ⅜	7 ½	6	3 ¾
17	4 ¼	4 ¼	4 ¼	4 ¼	4 ¾	5	3 ¼	5 ⅜	6 ¾	3 ⅜	6 ¾	5 ⅝	6 ¾	5 ⅝	2	6 ¾	5 ⅝	3 ⅛	7 ⅛	5 ⅝	3 ⅝
16	4	4	4	4	4 ½	4 ¾	3 ⅛	5	6 ⅜	3 ¼	6 ⅜	5 ⅜	6 ⅜	5 ⅜	1 ⅞	6 ⅜	5 ⅜	3	6 ⅝	5 ⅜	3 ⅜
15	3 ¾	3 ¾	3 ¾	3 ¾	4 ⅛	4 ⅜	2 ⅞	4 ⅝	6	3	6	5	6	5	1 ⅞	6	5	2 ¾	6 ¼	5	3 ¼
14	3 ½	3 ½	3 ½	3 ½	3 ⅞	4 ⅛	2 ¾	4 ⅜	5 ⅝	2 ¾	5 ⅝	4 ⅝	5 ⅝	4 ⅝	1 ¾	5 ⅝	4 ⅝	2 ⅝	5 ⅞	4 ⅝	3
13	3 ¼	3 ¼	3 ¼	3 ¼	3 ⅝	3 ⅞	2 ⅝	4	5 ¼	2 ⅝	5 ¼	4 ⅜	5 ¼	4 ⅜	1 ¾	5 ¼	4 ⅜	2 ⅜	5 ⅜	4 ⅜	2 ⅞
12	3	3	3	3	3 ¾	3 ½	2 ½	3 ¾	4 ¾	2 ⅜	4 ¾	4	4 ¾	4	1 ⅝	4 ¾	4	2 ¼	5	4	2 ⅝
11	2 ¾	2 ¾	2 ¾	2 ¾	3	3 ¼	2 ⅜	3 ⅜	4 ⅜	2 ¼	4 ⅜	3 ⅝	4 ⅜	3 ⅝	1 ⅝	4 ⅜	3 ⅝	2 ⅛	4 ⅝	3 ⅝	2 ½
10	2 ½	2 ½	2 ½	2 ½	2 ¾	3	2 ¼	3 ⅛	4	2 ⅛	4	3 ⅜	4	3 ⅜	1 ½	4	3 ⅜	2	4 ⅛	3 ⅜	
9							2 ⅛	2 ⅞	3 ⅝	2 ⅛	3 ⅝	3	3 ⅝	3	1 ½	3 ⅝	3	2	3 ¾	3	
8							1 ¾	2 ½	3 ¼	2	3 ½	2 ⅝	3 ¼	2 ⅝		3 ¼	2 ¾	1 ⅞	3 ⅜	2 ¾	
7							1	2 ⅛	2 ¾	2	2 ¾	2 ⅜	2 ¾	2 ⅜		2 ¾	2 ⅝	1 ⅞	2 ⅞	2 ⅝	
6							1	2	2 ⅝	1 ⅞	2 ⅜	2	2 ⅜	2		2 ⅜	2 ⅜	1 ¾	2 ½	2 ⅜	
5											2	1 ⅝	2			2			2 ⅛		
4																			1 ⅝		
3																			1 ¼		
2																			⅞		

From John Fincham, *On Masting Ships and Mastmaking* (3rd edition, London 1854)

Details of boat sails and rigging, 1794

A. RIGGING

Ships' longboats or launches are often rigged like small sloops or schooners.

Ships' pinnaces and rowing barges sometimes have lateen sails, and rig with a sliding-gunter, like houarios, or bend to yards, and hoist with haliards, that reeve through a sheave-hole in the mast-head: one end bends to the slings of the yard, on the fore-part of the mast, and the other end belays abaft the mast.

Sheets bend to the clue of the sail, and lead aft.

Spritsails, similar to those in sailing barges, are sometimes used.

Ships' cutters or yawls sometimes have lug-sails, and rig with a haliard, like the pinnace. Sheet and tack, like the lugger.

The necessary ropes belonging to these are: **the painter,** which splices round a thimble in the ringbolt within the bow.

The **sternfast** splices round a thimble in the ringbolt within the stern.

Fenders are made of worn cable-laid rope, doubled three or four times, and sewed together with spun-yarn thus: the rope is first doubled, and a laniard thrust through the bight, and a wall-knot crowned on the end: the ends are then brought up in the bight, and the four parts sewed together.

Rudder laniards: the ends are thrust through holes in the after part of the rudder, on contrary sides; and a double wall-knot, crowned, is made at the ends; the inner ends make fast on each quarter of the boat withinside.

Slings have a hook and thimble spliced in each end, with a long and short leg, by having a thimble seized in the bight at one-third the length.

B. MASTS

Sloops', smacks', hoys' and boats' masts from a middle-line are trimmed thus. The height of the partners is two-thirds the diameter, taking feet for inches, set up from the butt or heel, and there set off the given diameter as before. In the middle between the partners and the stop of the shrouds, thirty thirty-one parts of the given diameter; at the under part of the hounds seven-eighths; at the upper part, seven-tenths; and to have stops of one inch and a half, or two inches, on each side athwartships in proportion to the size of the mast. Topmast, in the middle between the stops, two-thirds of the given diameter; at the upper part, three-fifths; and the square head above the top-mast three-sevenths; and completed as the former.

Boats' masts, not sloop-fashion, are trimmed round from heel to head thus: strike a straight line along the middle, and set up the partners from the heel, which is the depth of the boat, and there set off the given diameter; then set up the whole length, and line it to two-thirds the diameter of the partners; with a sheave-hole its length clear of the stop for the haliards.

PROPORTIONS OF MASTS, YARDS, ETC, FOR SLOOPS, SMACKS AND HOYS

Proportional lengths

Mast and topmast in one, thrice and 3/4 the breadth of the vessel
Mast to the rigging-stop or hound 3/4 the whole length
Mast and topmast to the stop of the topmast 40/41 of the whole length
Topgallant mast to the rigging-stop 4/7 of the length of the mast
Boom 2/3 of the mast
Gaff 3/5 of the boom
Spread yard 5/8 of the mast
Crossjack yard 2/5 of the mast
Topsail yard 4/5 of the crossjack yard
Topgallant yard 5/6 of the topsail yard
Bowsprits 5/9 of the mast

Proportional diameters in fractional parts of an inch to every foot in length

Mast 1/4
Topgallant mast 3/8
Boom 3/16
Gaff 1/4
Spread yard 1/7
Crossjack yard 2/10
Topsail yard 2/10
Topgallant yard 1/8
Bowsprit 3/8

MASTS, YARDS, ETC, FOR BOATS

Long boats, sloop fashion, as above; but with lug-sails as follow.

Lengths

Mainmast twice and a half the breadth of the boat
Foremast 7/8 of the mainmast
Bowsprit 1/2 of the mainmast
Main yard 5/8 of the mainmast
Fore yard 5/8 of the foremast

Diameters in fractional parts of an inch to every foot in length
Mainmast 1/4
Foremast 1/4
Main yard 1/4
Fore yard 1/4
Bowsprit 5/8

LAUNCHES AND CUTTERS WITH LUG-SAILS

Lengths

Mainmast twice and 3/4 the breadth of the boat
Foremast 8/9 of the mainmast
Main yard 9/17 of the mainmast
Fore yard 9/17 of the foremast
Mizen mast 5/8 of the mainmast
Sprit 2 feet longer than the mizen mast
Outrigger 2/3 of the mizen mast

Diameters in fractional parts of an inch to every foot in length

Mainmast 1/4
Foremast 1/4
Main yard 1/4
Fore yard 1/4
Mizen mast 1/4
Sprit 1/7
Outrigger 3/7

LAUNCHES AND CUTTERS WITH SETTEE-SAILS

Length of the main yard, thrice and 1/2 the breadth of the vessel
Mainmast 4/7 of the main yard
Foremast 17/18 of the mainmast
Fore yard 9/10 of the main yard
Diameter of the masts 3/8 of an inch to every foot in length
Yards 1/4of an inch to every foot in the length

BARGES AND PINNACES WITH LATEEN-SAILS

Length of the masts twice the breadth of the boat and 8 inches added
Topmasts the length of the mast and 1/9 more
Scarf to the lower-mast 1/4 of its length

Diameter of the masts 5/16 of an inch
to every foot in length
Topmasts 2/10 of an inch to every foot
in length

BARGES, PINNACES AND YAWLS WITH SPRITSAILS

Length of the main and fore masts
twice and 1/4 the breadth of the vessel
Sprits 1/8 more than the mast
Diameters of the masts 1/4 of an inch
to every foot in the length
Sprits 1/8 of an inch to every foot in
the length

C. SAIL-MAKING

BOAT'S SETTEE SAIL

This sail is quadrilateral, and made of
canvas No 7 or 8. The head is bent to a
lateen yard, which hangs obliquely to
the mast at one-third of its length, and
extends within six inches of the cleats.

The cloth at the tack is cut goring
to the nock, and the bunt is of the
depth of the reef; which is one-fifth of
the depth of the leech. The leech is
five-sixths of the length of the head.

The length of the head, divided by
the number of cloths in it, gives the
length of each gore. The foot is cut
with a circular sweep, after the sail is
sewed together.

Two small holes are made in each
cloth along the head; and holes are
made across the sail, on each seam, at
one-fifth of the depth of the leech
from the foot, for the reef. A small
reef-cringle is made on the after-leech-
rope, and cringles are made at the
nock and peak.

BOAT'S LATEEN SAIL

This sail is triangular, and made of
canvas No 7 or 8. It is so called from
its head being bent to the lateen yard,
which hangs obliquely to the mast at
one-third of its length, extending
within six inches of the cleats.

The length of the head, divided by
the number of cloths, gives the length
of the gore on each cloth. The foot is
cut square.

Two small holes are made in each
cloth along the head, through which
the lacings are reeved.

This sail, when the head of it (then
called the fore-leech) is laced to a mast
and topmast, is called a sliding-gunter-
sail; the topmast being made to slide

down the mast by means of hoops.

It is likewise called a shoulder-of-
mutton-sail, when laced by the fore-
leech to a single mast.

BOAT'S LUG SAIL

This sail is quadrilateral, and made of
canvas No 7 or 8. The head is bent to a
yard, which hangs obliquely to the
mast at one third of its length, and
extends within four inches of the
cleats.

Two or three cloths are gored on
the fore leech, and an even gore of six
inches per cloth is made on the head.
The foot is gored with a sweep; the
cloth at the clue being cut with a
three-inch short gore, the next cloth is
square, and the cloths from thence to
the tack are gored at the rate of six or
eight inches per cloth.

The fore leech is as deep as the
length of the head, and the after leech
is longer than the fore leech by nearly
half the depth of the fore leech.

Two small holes are made in each
cloth in the head.

This sail has two reefs parallel with
the foot, the upper one is half way up
the fore leech, and the other is equally
distant from that and the foot.
Sometimes reef-bands three or four
inches broad are put on at the reefs,
but when these are not used, a small
hole is made in every seam instead of
them.

Small cringles are made on the
leeches at each reef; earing-cringles are
made at the nock and peak; and ten or
twelve strands in the length of the rope
are seized at the tack and clue.

BOAT'S SPRITSAILS

These sails are quadrilateral, and made
of canvas No 7 or 8, the fore leeches
are attached to their respective masts
by lacings, reeved through holes made
in them; and the heads are elevated and
extended by sprits, or small yards, that
cross the sail diagonally, from the mast
to the peak; the lower end of the sprit,
rests in a wreath or collar of rope
called a snotter, which encircles the
mast at the foot of the sail.

The fore leeches of the main and
fore spritsails are the depth of the mast
within 12 inches of the gunwale, and
have one or two gored cloths. The
heads of them have an even gore of 12
or 14 inches per cloth.

The fore leech of the mizen spritsail
is the depth of the mast, so as to clear
the gunwale; and is square. The head
has an even gore of 11 inches per cloth.

Small holes are made in the fore
leeches: those in the main and fore
spritsails are one yard, and those in the
mizen are three-quarters of a yard
asunder. Holes are also made in the
seams, across the sail, at one-fifth of the
depth of the after leech from the foot,
for the reef.

Ten or twelve turns or twists of the
strands in the length of the rope is
seized, to form bights, at the tack,
nock, peak and clue.

BOAT'S FORESAIL

This sail is triangular, and made of canvas No 8. The leech is of the same
depth as the fore leech of the fore
spritsail, and the foot is made wide
enough to spread from the stem to the
mast.

The depth of the fore part, or hoist,
divided by the number of cloths, gives
the length of each gore. The foot is cut
square.

Two inches of slack cloth should be
taken up with the rope in every yard
in the depth of the hoist.

BOAT'S JIB

This sail is triangular, and made of
canvas No 8. The leech is of the same
depth as the leech of the fore sail, and
the foot is as wide as the length of the
bowsprit.

The depth of the fore part, or hoist,
divided by the number of cloths, gives
the length of each gore. The foot is cut
with a sweep, at the rate of six or seven
inches per cloth, with a short gore to
the clue.

Two inches of slack-cloth should be
taken up with the rope in every yard in
the hoist.

From David Steel, *The Elements and Practice
of Rigging and Seamanship* (London 1794).

Chapter 5 COMING OF STEAM

At first glance the Royal Navy would appear to have begun the intro-duction of steam boats in 1822, when the Admiralty approved the purchase for £618.15.0 of a small steam ferry-boat at Rio de Janeiro, by Captain William Fitzwilliam Owen of the *Leven*, to serve as a ten-der for the purpose of assisting him in the survey of the eastern coast of Africa.[167] However, if we look further into this matter we find that the boat was bought 'without her apparatus'. In any case she would not come into the category of a ship's boat for she drew about six feet of water and, being too large to hoist in, was towed across the Atlantic. Actually the first steam boat tried in the Royal Navy seems to have been one supplied to the *Maeander* in 1847.[168] In 1850 orders were given for it to be disposed of in China.[169]

There was then a gap of several years until 1864, when six launches of the usual pattern were ordered to be fitted with boilers and twin-screw engines. They were supplied to the *Bombay*, *Achilles*, *Isis*, *Vindictive*, *Investigator* and *Victoria*.[170] Immediately a general request for these boats arose and in the

By the time of the 'Crimean' war with Russia in 1854-56, much of the front-line fleet was driven by steam, but all the boats were still rowed or sailed. In the Baltic, the amphibious operations that supported operations like the bombardment of Sveaborg depicted in this John Wilson Carmichael painting were undertaken by boats that would have been familiar to Nelson, and not very novel to Drake. (*BHC0636*)

following years more and more were ordered and their use was gradually extended.

The boats were the ordinary open launches with boiler and engines fitted to them and in 1867 a suggestion was made that a canvas hood should be place over the fore part of the boat to prevent seas breaking inboard and putting out the boiler fires.[171] In this same year a 36ft steam pinnace was ordered from White of Cowes for trial and from this date steam pinnaces in a variety of lengths appeared. They were shortly followed by steam cutters, and by 1877 all three types of steam boats were common.

In the 1890s experiments led to the 56ft steam pinnace coming into use. Though officially known as steam pinnaces these were always called picket boats in the Navy, for their original principal purpose was intended to be the patrolling of the mouth of harbours for the protection of ships anchored therein from the attacks of torpedo boats. Based on earlier designs of smaller steam pinnaces these boats had a small fore-peak for stowing a chain cable; then a crew compartment, followed by boiler-room, engine-room and cabin, the last having doors facing aft into open stern-sheets. Except for the last named, the boat was decked and there was space to walk fore and aft on either side of the raised metal casing which covered the boiler and engine-rooms. The wheel was situated in a narrow gangway between the after side

Right By the 1880s the rapidly advancing technology of steam machinery meant that quite small boats could be mechanically propelled. This 21ft steam gig was powered by an experimental compound surface condensing engine of Kingdon's patent. It is dated Devonport Yard 30 August 1883. (*BS (f) 2*)

Dated 18 November 1868, this draught shows the newly adopted canvas screen forward. It is a rather poignant document, as it is marked '30ft life gig for HMS *Captain*', the turret ship that capsized in a Biscay gale in September 1870; the boats went down with the ship and only 17 men of 490 on board were saved. (*BS(f) 1*)

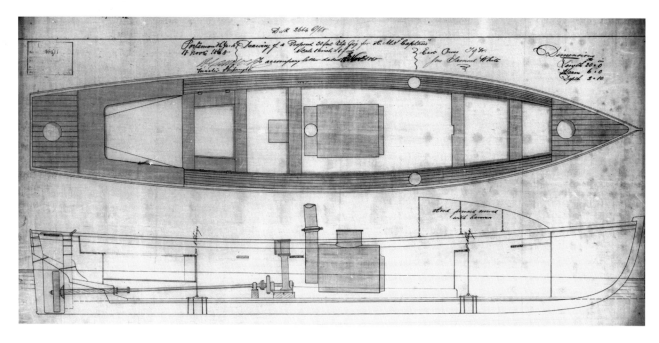

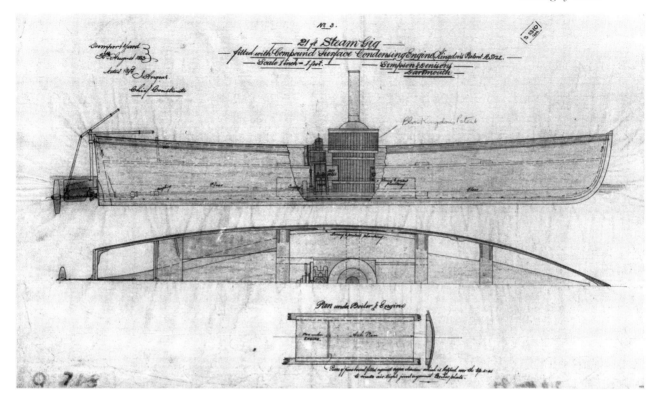

Hoisting out the battleship *Royal Sovereign*'s smaller steam pinnace in about 1897. Ratings appear to be preparing the picket boat on the inner set of cradles to follow; there are also a pair of conventional davits swung out with boats lowered. (*59/6*)

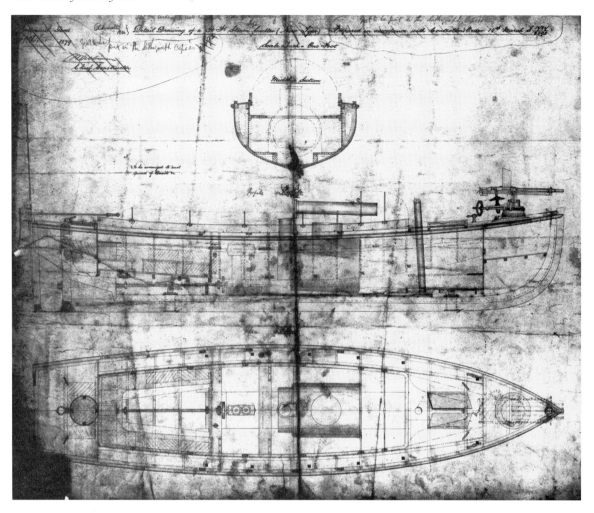

of the engine-room casing and the fore side of the cabin top. The boat had two thin funnels, placed abreast.

Above the crew quarters there was fixed the steel frustrum of a cone surmounted by a universal interrupted ring on which either a 3-pounder or a Maxim gun could be mounted. A second ring, intended to take a Maxim, was fixed to the cabin top. Two brass plates were let into the deck on each side and to these could be fitted dropping gear for 14in torpedoes.

The last ships to whom these boats were supplied were the *Lord Nelson* and *Agamemnon*: later ships were supplied instead with 50ft boats. These boats were of very similar build with a single funnel, but the gun-mounting forward was omitted as it had been decided that quick-firing guns should no longer be fitted in boats. When war broke out in 1914 steam boats were again used to patrol the entrance to the fleet anchorage and for this it was deemed necessary that they should carry 3-pounders. This made it necessary for the 50ft boats to be fitted with a platform of baulks of timber to take a conical gun support.

This rather battered draught shows the new type 30ft steam (life) cutter introduced in 1879. The midship section shows the buoyancy chambers along the sides, and a new feature is the fitting for a multi-barrelled Nordenfelt machine gun forward. (*BS(b)14*)

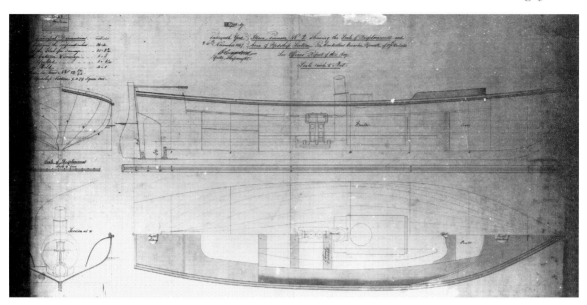

The original draught of Steam Pinnace No 2, one of the first 36ft steam boats. It is dated Portsmouth Yard 26 November 1867, and is noted as a response to the Controller's circular of 17 December 1866. *(BS(e)4)*

The earliest reference that I have been able to find for a steam boat being supplied exclusively for the use of a flag officer was in 1882 when a steam cutter was ordered to be specially prepared for the use of Rear-Admiral Sir William Nathan Wrighte Hewett, Commander-in-Chief of the East Indies station with his flag in the *Euryalus*. This was quickly followed by a steam barge for Vice-Admiral Sir William Montagu Dowell, commanding the Channel Squadron in the *Minotaur*.[172]

The use of steam barges now spread rapidly and a distinct type of steam boat appeared for this service. The first of these were 32ft and 40ft boats, which were developed in the late 1890s, and these were followed in the next decade by 45ft boats. While generally following the design of the steam pinnaces these boats had the distinctive feature of a long overhanging counter instead of a square transom.

The First World War marks a period in the history of the boats of men-of-war. Ideas changed. No longer must boats under oars or sail be used in preference to steam boats in order to conserve the latter's fuel. Convenience and speed were now the order of the day. This led to the rapid introduction and spread in the use of boats with internal combustion engines. Experiments with these had been begun early in the century and it had at one time been intended that the *Dreadnought* should have two 50ft motor pinnaces in lieu of picket boats.[173] In the latter years of the war sailing launches and sailing pinnaces were being fitted with motors. The ideas behind these turned full circle. As with the first steam launches these motor launches were first completely open, then a canvas canopy appeared and finally a wooden top enclosing the engine and part of the stern sheets.

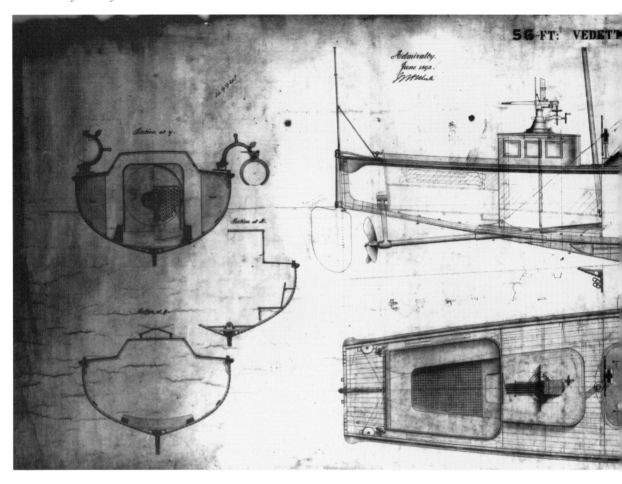

56-FT: VEDETTE

Above Official draught of the 56ft vedette boat (or pinnace), dated Admiralty June 1892. It shows a 3-pounder forward and a five-barrelled rifle-calibre Nordenfelt machine gun aft, as well as torpedo release gear on either broadside amidships. This model has a single funnel rather than twins abreast. (*BS(r)1*)

Left The battleship *Resolution* in 1905, hoisting out the picket boat. The smaller steam pinnace is already in the water alongside, but the rest of the ship's outfit are pulling boats. (*N422*)

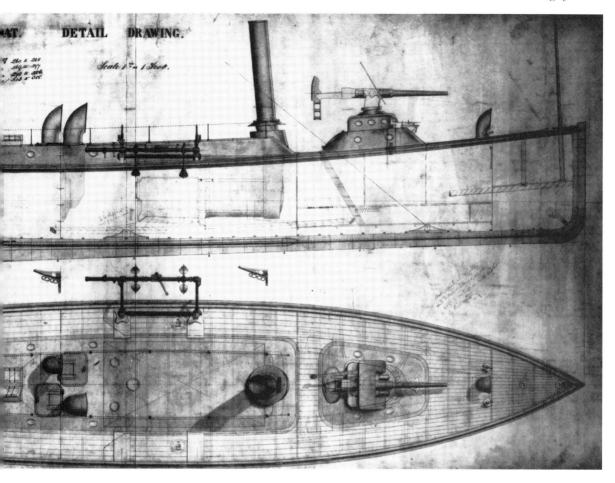

DETAIL DRAWING.

Scale 1" = 1 foot.

Picket boats were heavy and even the most robust derrick could not always cope, as demonstrated by this accident to the armoured cruiser *Hampshire* in 1913. However, it reveals the deck layout of the boat very clearly. (*A6452*)

Left Boat stowage in the battleship *Prince of Wales* at Dover in 1908. The 45ft steam pinnace and picket boat dominate the boat deck. (*N6946*)

Boat establishments for ironclads, about 1870

Boat type	Construction	Rig
BOOM BOATS		
2 eighteen-oared launches, double-banked★	Diagonal	Two masts, standing lugs & staysail
1 fourteen-oared pinnace, double-banked	Diagonal	Two masts, standing lugs & staysail
CUTTERS		
2 twelve-oared cutters, double-banked	Clinker	Two masts, dipping lugs
1 ten- or eight- oared cutter, double-banked	Clinker	Two masts, dipping lugs
GIGS OR WHALERS		
1 six-oared captain's galley, single-banked+	Clinker	Single standing lug
2 five-oared whalers, single banked	Clinker	Single standing lug
(or 1 whaler and 1 four-oared gig)		
SMALL CRAFT		
1 dinghy		
1 coppering punt	Clinker	Single standing lug
IN ADDITION, FOR FLAGSHIPS		
1 fourteen-oared barge or extra gig	Clinker	Single standing lug
(sometimes both)		

★ One of the launches could be converted to steam propulsion: the twin propeller shafts were permanent, but the boiler/engine assembly could be added quickly.

+ In the official stores list the galley was referred to as a gig.
From G A Ballard, *The Black Battlefleet* (Lymington 1980), pp.57-58; it also details a number of non-standard outfits.

Chapter 6 ARMING BOATS

From very early times, whenever boats were used for warlike purposes their crews were armed with small arms. Sir Thomas Allin mentions covering fire from boats for a watering party in 1661.[174]

In January 1737/8 when the *Centurion* was ordered to the East Coast of Africa, Captain George Anson was advised to apply for four swivels to mount in her longboat for its protection while watering,[175] and four years later the launches of the *Burford* and *Suffolk*, which had been supplied to replace their longboats were ordered to be fitted with stocks for mounting six swivels, before the ships sailed for the West Indies.[176]

In 1795 instructions were given that the launches of certain ships of the line were to be fitted with slides for mounting carronades,[177] and in the following year this order was extended to all launches.[178] The carronades supplied were to be 24-pounders for launches of ships of 100, 80 or 76 guns,

A detail from de Loutherbourg's dramatic rendition of the landings in Aboukir Bay in March 1801, showing a launch carronade in action. These were standard fitting in all warships from 1795. (*1738*)

Above Boats were always considered an extension of a warship's reach - much like the multi-purpose helicopter of a modern frigate – and as such were employed in a number of roles for which an armament was useful. One of the first of these was the support of amphibious landings, where shoal water often prevented big ships getting close enough inshore for effective fire support – Serres' painting of the Havana landings in June 1762 provides an illustration. Boats armed with marines, then swivel guns, and finally carronades, could give a degree of close support otherwise lacking. (*BHC0409*)

Right During the course of the Napoleonic Wars, the Royal Navy became ever more adept and aggressive in its use of boats for cutting-out expeditions, like this attack on a flotilla of French gunboats by the sloop *Procris* in 1811. To facilitate such operations, even barges and pinnaces were armed with small carronades; this was officially adopted in the Channel Fleet in 1811 but was the unofficial practice elsewhere and earlier. (*6296*)

18-pounders for those of 90, 74 and 64-gun ships, and 12-pounders for those of ships of 20 to 50 guns and of large sloops.

The slides fitted originally ran the full length of the boat, so that the carronade might be used at either end, but during the latter part of the French Wars it was shortened to extend aft only to the third or fourth thwart. At one third of its length from the fore end the slide was hinged so that, if the thwart were unshipped, the end could be inclined down, enabling the carronade to be slid down into the bottom of the boat to improve her stability when it was not required. In bad weather it was very necessary to get the weight low in the boat.

In 1823 the launches of ships of the line were ordered to be fitted with slides to take an 18-pounder carronade at each end, while the launches of frigates and all barges and pinnaces were to carry a single 12-pounder.[179] The fitting of 12-pounder carronades in the barges and pinnaces of the Channel Fleet had been authorised in 1811.[180]

In 1828 the arming of boats was again under consideration by the Admiralty and some modifications were made to the orders of 1823. The launches of frigates were now to carry two 12-pounder carronades instead of one, and Congreve rocket launchers were to be carried in all boats smaller than launches and pinnaces. A suggestion had been made that a 24-pounder howitzer would be a better armament for launches than the two 18-pounder carronades and pending a decision on this point captains of battleships might arm their launches with howitzers or carronades as they preferred.[181] During the next quarter of a century we read of 24-pounder howitzers being fitted in the boats of various ships.[182]

By about 1840 it was becoming the usual practice to use the same guns alternatively as boat or field guns.[183] This led to the gradual introduction of 6-pounder guns for boats. A 12-pounder breech-loader was coming into use. About 1861 the 20-pounder breech-loading Armstrongs started to be supplied to ships,[184] the 20-pounder for the larger launches and the 9-

Congreve rockets were another weapon easily adapted to boats, since there was no recoil to absorb – a problem with conventional guns in small craft. Rocket boats were used against Boulogne and other would-be invasion ports in 1805-6, but came to the fore in the operations on the American coast during the War of 1812. (*C1464*)

Among the advantages claimed for John Cow's launch was the ease with which field artillery could be put ashore, without the necessity to dismantle the carriage. From his booklet *Remarks on the Manner of Fitting Boats for Ships of War and Transports*, third edition, published in 1843. (*E0380-2*)

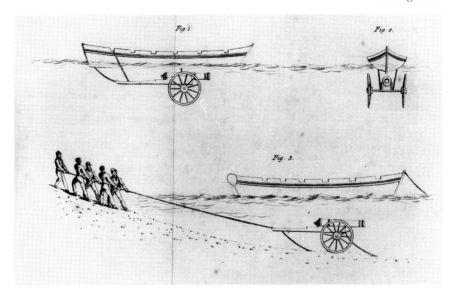

pounder for barges and pinnaces. The 9-pounder was intended to replace the 12-pounder.[185] The Armstrongs were by no means so satisfactory as had been claimed for them and by 1865 opinion in the Service was already swinging against breech-loaders.[186] It was decided to fit no more 20-pounder Armstrongs but to retain for the time being the 12-pounder breech-loader.

Variations of the muzzle-loading 7-pounder used by the Army as a mountain gun were now introduced into the Royal Navy as boat and field guns and were closely followed by a muzzle-loading 9-pounder.

By 1873 pulling launches were each carrying either a 12-pounder 8cwt breech-loading gun or a 9-pounder 8cwt muzzle-loader, while each pinnace carried a 9-pounder 6cwt, either the Armstrong breech-loader or a muzzle-loader.[187] Two years later the 7-pounder muzzle-loader was being fitted in steam pinnaces and pulling launches.

By 1884 the 9-pounder Armstrong and the 12-pounder breech-loader had dropped out of use. Steam cutters had been added to the list of boats carrying 7-pounders, while among pulling cutters this gun was fitted only in the 28ft boat. Other cutters had either a 24-pounder rocket tube or a 0.45in machine gun, the latter being either a Gatling (which had been introduced into the Royal Navy in 1873) or a Gardner (introduced 1882).[188]

By 1885 the Nordenfelt had also been introduced into the Royal Navy and came in two types. There were a twin-barrelled version of 1in bore and a 0.45in five-barrelled one. The 0.45in Nordenfelt became an alternative to the other two machine guns. Steam launches and steam pinnaces were now to carry guns, the former a 9-pounder 8cwt as in a pulling boat of the same type, the latter either a 7-pounder, or a 1in Nordenfelt or a machine gun of any type. The 28ft steam cutter might now have either the 7-pounder or a

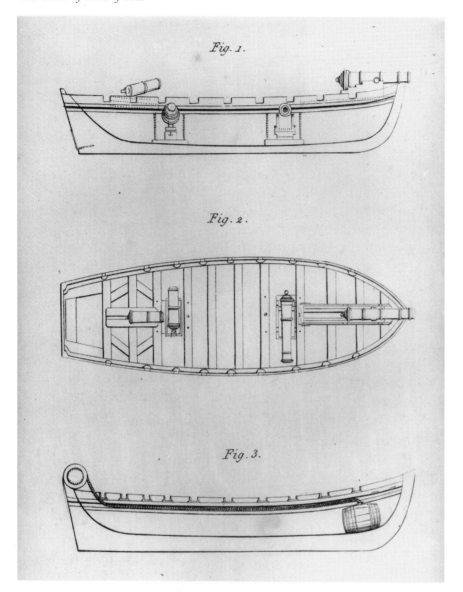

Fig. 1.

Fig. 2.

Fig. 3.

John Cow's demonstration of how his launch might carry a long gun forward and a carronade aft. The usual method of stowage involved a slide which could be hinged at the end so that the carronade could be slid down onto the bottom boards. From Cow's booklet *Remarks on the Manner of Fitting Boats for Ships of War and Transports*, third edition, published in 1843. (*E0396*)

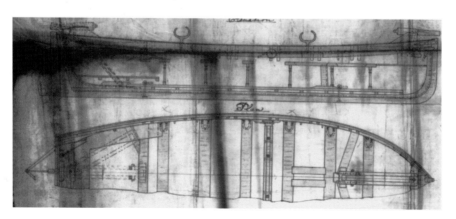

A draught of a 28ft pinnace with a 7-pounder muzzle-loader fore and aft. This version of the army's mountain gun was mounted on a traversing slide. (*Bu(e)34*)

0.45in machine gun, while the use of rockets in boats was discontinued.

In this year of 1885, 3- and 6-pounder quick-firing guns were added to the guns available to the Navy. These were responsible for more proposed changes. Steam pinnaces of 37ft and upwards should have one or two of the new 3-pounders, 30ft steam cutters should have a 1in Nordenfelt in the bow and a 0.45in in the stern. Smaller steam cutters and pulling cutters would carry a 0.45in Nordenfelt only; pulling launches would exchange the 9-pounder muzzle-loader for a 6-pounder quick-firer. The Gatling was given up as being too liable to jam to be reliable.[189] These proposals did not however come into being for some time. In 1889 of the steam pinnaces only some of those of 48ft and 52ft had acquired the 3-pounder, some of those of 48ft and under still having their 7-pounder muzzle-loaders. All had a 0.45in Gardner or Nordenfelt in addition. Pulling launches had failed to get the 6-pounder quick-firer, but had the 3-pounder instead, accompanied by a 0.45in machine gun.[190]

By 1892 only the 37ft steam pinnace was left with the 7-pounder muzzle-loader and this remained in service until about 1900. In the early 1890s the 0.45in Maxim began to replace the Gardners and Nordenfelts, which were gone by the end of the century.[191] Another innovation to start the new century was a new 12-pounder 8cwt quick-firer fitted in 42ft pulling launches.[192] At the same time the 0.45in Maxim was giving way to the 0.303in.

The original reason behing the introduction of the quick-firing guns for boats arose from the growing danger from torpedo boats. It was thought that when a fleet was at anchor it would put our a screen of armed boats and, if suitably armed, these would be able to sink any torpedo boat before it was able to get within torpedo range. By 1907 torpedo boats had increased so much in size that the guns which could be carried by boats were no longer

A draught of a 40ft steam pinnace, annotated 'Nos 287 to 310', undated but about 1895. The boat has a 3-pounder forward and a five-barrelled 0.45in Nordenfelt machine gun aft. With regard to the latter, a note says 'Provision to is be made for fighting gun in middle line position'. Spar torpedo gear is also shown. *(BS(e)12a)*

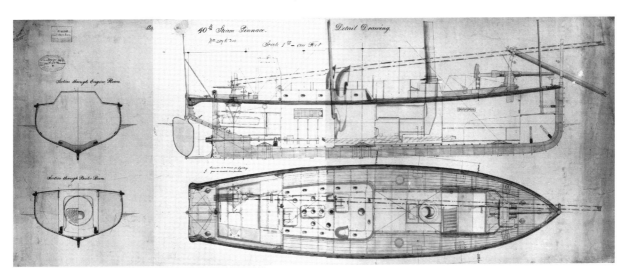

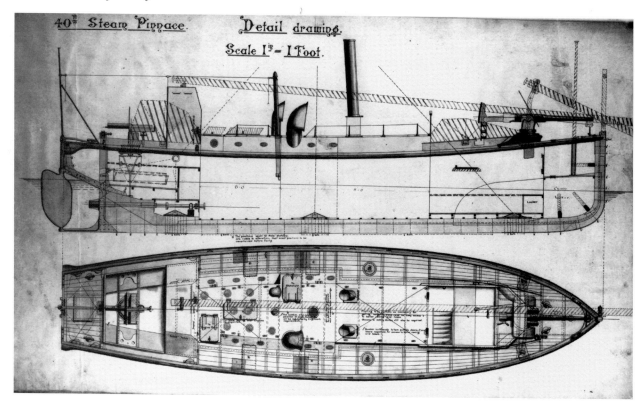

Above A slightly later 40ft steam pinnace (probably post-1896) showing a Maxim gun aft. This is on the centreline, which required moving the steering position, now protected by a splinter-proof screen. (*BS(e)12d*)

Two 12-pounder guns, their field carriages and ammunition loaded aboard the launch of the First Class cruiser *Terrible*. They are about to be towed ashore by the steam pinnace as reinforcements to British naval forces at Tientsin in July 1900. (*C7225/15*)

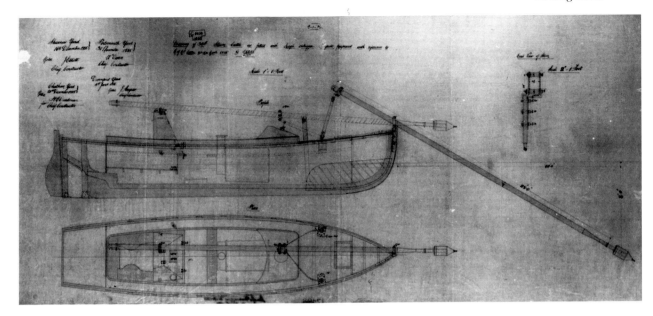

A single outrigger torpedo fitted to a 30ft steam cutter, 1885. The plan view, and light line in profile, shows the stowed position, and the heavy line in the profile the spar torpedo as deployed – the warhead is then 20ft ahead of the boat and 8ft below the surface. *(BS(b)28)*

large enough to be effective. It was accordingly decided that no boats built in future should be fitted for anything except machine guns.[193]

Since the fitting of quick-firing guns had been introduced a universal type of mounting had been used so that they could be readily installed in a special holding-down ring.

Guns and rocket launchers were not the only weapons fitted to boats. In the 1860s all large steam boats could carry outrigger torpedoes, otherwise known as spar-torpedoes. These outrigger torpedoes were carried in a pair of crutches on each side. When required for use the spar was slid forwards and depressed so that the 100lb charge at the forward end was fifteen to eighteen feet before the boat and ten feet below the surface. It could then

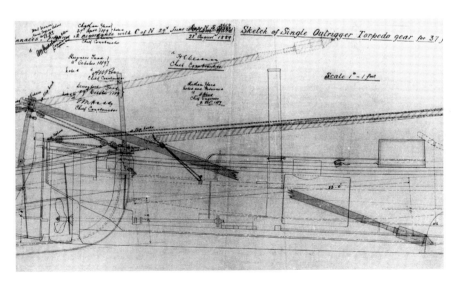

Detail sketches (overlapping bow and stern) of the rigging of a spar torpedo for a 37ft steam pinnace, 1889. *(BS(e)23d)*

be detonated against the enemy's side without damaging the boat. It was also suggested that these outrigger torpedoes with 30lb or 40lb charges could even be used in gigs.[194] About 1875 the automobile torpedo having come into service, dropping gear was introduced. A 14in torpedo could be suspended from a pair of davits at the side of the boat and having been trained onto the target by pointing the boat could be released. This torpedo dropping gear replaced the spar torpedoes and was still in use in 1914.

An early form of steam picket boat, with twin funnels, armed with two Whitehead 'automobile' torpedoes in dropping cradles. Such boats gave every major ship a limited smooth-water torpedo boat capability. (*N10887*)

Above Although apparently suicidal at first glance, practical experience in the American Civil War and later in the Russo-Turkish War of 1877 proved that the spar torpedo could be effective in the right circumstances. As a result the Royal Navy assiduously practised both attack and defence with the weapon. This lively oil painting by Eduardo de Martino (1838-1912) depicts a fleet review in which steam boats launch a spar torpedo attack on HMS *Edinburgh*, protected by net defences boomed out from the hull. (*BHC1674*)

NOTES

1. Sir Nicholas Harris Nicolas, *A History of the Royal Navy* Vol. II (London 1847), pp174, 477.

2. Alan Moore, 'Accounts and Inventories of John Starlyng, Clerk of the King's Ships to Henry IV', *Mariner's Mirror* IV (1914), pp20-26, 167-173.

3. Exchequer Accounts, Public Record Office E 101/25/7.

4. M Oppenheim, *Naval Accounts and Inventories of Henry VII* (London 1896), pp 192-193.

5. Nathaniel Boteler, or Butler, is usually considered to have written his dialogues originally shortly before 1634, in which date he took one version with him to America, but I suggest that it is more likely that he began to write more than ten years earlier. This would explain some discrepancies with other writers of the period. The versions which have survived are:

A1 *Six Dialogues about Sea Services.* Printed in 1685 from a manuscript which has disappeared.

A2 *Colloquia Maritima or Six Dialogues about Sea Services.* A reprint of A1.

B Bodleian Library, Rawlinson MS A 463. This differs little from A1.

C British Museum. Sloane MS No 758. This is dated 1634 and is the copy which Boteler took to America in that year.

D British Museum, Harleian MS No 1341. A revision of C.

E British Museum, Sloane MS No 2449.

F *Boteler's Dialogues.* Edited by W G Perrin from E and published by the Navy Records Society (London 1929).
Quotations and references in the present book are from A1.

6. Note 4, p259.

7. Note 4, p321.

8. August Jal, *Glossaire Nautique*, 1848.

9. Note 2.

10. Naval Historical Library, Ministry of Defence, MSS 12.

11. State Papers, Charles I, Public Record Office, SP 16/48.

12. M Oppenheim, *A History of the Administration of the Royal Navy and of Merchant Shipping in relation to the Royal Navy* (London 1896), p339.

13. Sir Henry Mainwaring, *The Seamans Dictionary, 1644*, Navy Records Society edition (London 1920), Vol II, p105.

14. Note 5(A1), p246.

15. (a) Bodleian Library, Tanner 296 and Tanner 297; National Maritime Museum, Dartmouth Papers.
(b) *The Journals of Sir Thomas Allin*, Navy Records Society edition, (London 1939), Vol I, p17.

16. Master's Log Book of the *Phoenix* 1684-1687, Public Records Office, Adm 51/3933.

17. R D Merriman (ed), *The Sergison Papers* (London 1960), p310.

18. Thomas Riley Blanckley, *The Naval Expositer* (London 1750), p14.

19. Rear-Admiral Sir R Massie Blomfield, 'Man of War Boats', *Mariner's Mirror*, I (1911), pp235-240; Vol. II (1912), pp7-9. Reference here to p239.

20. Sir Walter Raleigh. *His Apologie for his Voyage to Guiana*, (London 1650), p5.

21. Sir Walter Raleigh. *The discoverie of the large rich and bewtiful Empyre of Guiana*. 1596, Argonaut Press edition, (London 1928), pp35, 37, 41, 45.

22. Admiralty to Navy Board, Public Record Office, Adm 2/194, p175.

23. Admiralty to Navy Board, Public Record Office, Adm 2/181, pp99-100.

24. Admiralty to Navy Board, Public Record Office, Adm 2/182, p34.

25. Admiralty to Navy Board, Public Record Office, Adm 2/186, p49.

26. William Falconer. *An Universal Dictionary of the Marine.* (London 1769).

27. William Burney. *A New Universal Dictionary of the Marine.* (London 1815).

28. Navy Board Minutes, 10 & 15 September 1762, Public Record Office, Adm 106/2576.

29. Note 5(F), p197.

30. George Malcolm Thomson. *Sir Francis Drake.* (London 1972). p60.

31. Note 18.

32. Note 26.

33. Captain Walter Stirling to Navy Board, 1 March 1769, Public Record Office, Adm 106/1183.

34. Logbook of Captain of the *Salisbury*, 7 September 1722, Public Record Office, Adm 51/842.

35. India Office Library, P/Range 341/5.

36. Logbook of Captain of the *Lyon*, 16 October 1722, Public Record Office, Adm 51/538.

37. Captain Andrew Snape Hamond to Navy Board, 4 & 5 January 1771, Public Record Office, Adm 106/1198.

38. Note 5 (A1), p249.

39. John Smith. *The Sea-mans Grammar.* (London 1627), Chap vi, p26.

40. Note 5 (A1), p247.

41. Note 13, p103.

42. Note 15. Entry for 1 March 1667/8. Note 15(b), Vol II, p10.

43. Log-book of Captain of the *Hunter*, Public Record Office, Adm 51/3870, 13 December 1679.

44. Public Record Office, Foreign Accounts 21 Henry VI.G dorso. Quoted by *Oxford English Dictionary* but not checked.

45. Note 21, p36.

46. Instead of following Note 5(A1) which has already been quoted in this context at reference 38, I have here followed another version of Boteler's *Dialogues* quoted by Sir R Massie Blomfield, Note 19, p239.

47. Note 15. Entries for the 10, 12 & 13 January 1660/1 and 4 May & 2 August 1661. Note 15(b). Vol I, pp17, 34, 43.

48. Note 18.

49. Note 15.

50. Note 15. Entries for 3 May 1662. Note 15(b), Vol II, p75.

51. National Maritime Museum, NM 109.

52. Naval Historical Library, Ministry of Defence, MSS.9.

53. Navy Board Orders to Dockyards, Public Record Office, Adm 106/3551, No 2.

54. Admiralty to Navy Board, Public Record Office, Adm 2/181, pp62-3.

55. Admiralty to Navy Board, Public Record Office, Adm 2/182, p75.

56. Captain James Gunman to Admiralty, 3 April 1709, Public Record Office, Adm 1/824.

57. Note 56. Letter dated 18 April 1709.

58. Note 56. Letter dated 23 October 1709. Captain Gunman wrote yet another letter dated 3 December 1709.

59. Officers who complained to the Admiralty that they could not hoist their longboats included the following (references in the Public Record Office):
1708 Captain Henry Lawson of the *Pearle* Adm 2/188, p25.
1709 Captain Michael Sansome of the *Mary* galley Adm 2/188, p78.
1710 Commander Edmond Hooke of the *Jamaica* sloop Adm 2/189, p520.

60. Navy Board to Admiralty, 25 October 1709. Public Record Office, Adm 1/3612.

61. Admiralty to Navy Board, Public Record Office, Adm 2/437, p62.

62. Navy Board Minutes, 6 October 1780, Public Record Office, Adm 106/2604.

63. Note 18.

64. Deal Letter Book, 29 September 1712, Public Record Office, Adm 106/3252.

65. Captain John Aldred to Navy Board, 17 September 1712, Public Record Office, Adm 106/671.

66. Note 64. Letter dated 20 May 1720.

67. Log-book of Captain of the *Lyon*, 22 April 1722, Public Record Office, Adm 51/538.

68. Admiralty to Navy Board, Public Record Office, Adm 2/200, p457.

69. Navy Board Minutes, Public Record Office, Adm 106/2554.

70. Commodore George Anson to Navy Board, 20 July 1742, Public Record Office, Adm 106/916.

71. Richard Walter, *A Voyage Round the World in the Years MDCCXL, I, II, III, IV* (London 1748), pp251, 257, 275, 276.

72. Navy Board Orders to Portsmouth, National Maritime Museum, POR/A.23, 16 September 1766.

73. Navy Board to Admiralty, 17 March 1714/5, Public Record Office, Adm 1/3626. Admiralty to Navy Board, 18 March 1714/5, Public Record Office, Adm 2/193, p183.

74. John Cow, *Remarks on the Manner of fitting Boats for Ships of War and Transports* (3rd ed 1843).

75. Note 68.

76. Captains George Anson and Daniel Kidd to Navy Board, 20 July 1740, Public Record Office, Adm 106/916 & Adm 106/923.

77. Captain Walter Stirling to Navy Board, 1 March 1769, Public Record Office, Adm 106/1183.

78. Navy Board Orders to Dockyards, Public Record Office, Adm 106/2508, No 546.

79. Navy Board Order to Dockyards, Public Record Office, Adm 106/2508, No 707.

80. Lord Colvill to Admiralty, Public Record Office, Adm 1/428, pp425-426.

81. Navy Board to Portsmouth, 18 July 1769. National Maritime Museum, POR/A.24. Navy Board Minutes, 18 July 1769, Public Record Office, Adm 106/2583.

82. Navy Board Order to Dockyards, Public Record Office, Adm 106/2508, No 579.

83. Navy Board Minutes, 19 July 1781, Public Record Office, Adm 106/2605.

84. Navy Board Order to Dockyards, Public Record Office, Adm 106/2508, No 1082.

85. Note 18.

86. J J Moore, *The British Mariner's Vocabulary or Universal Dictionary of Technical Terms and Sea Phrases* (London 1801). The second edition of 1805 prefixes the title with the words: *The Midshipman's or*

87. Note 15(b). Vol I, pp44, 51.

88. Captain Richard Norris to Navy Board, 11 April 1740, Public Record Office, Adm 106/923.

89. Captain Edward Boscawen to Admiralty, 27 July 1742, Public Record Office, Adm 1/1478.

90. Deptford Letter Book, 2 August 1742, Public Record Office, Adm 106/3503.

91. Admiralty to Navy Board, 24 August 1742, Public Record Office, Adm 2/203, p234.

92. Navy Board Minutes, 24 August 1742, Public Record Office, Adm 106/2557.

93. Captain Franklin Lushington to Admiralty, 4 September 1742, Public Records Office, Adm 1/2041.

94. Admiralty Minutes, 17 September 1742, Public Record Office, Adm 3/46.

95. Navy Board Minutes, 2 July 1762, Public Record Office, Adm 106/2576.

96. Navy Board Minutes, 8 January 1771, Public Record Office, Adm 106/2584.

97. Navy Board Order to Dockyards, Public Record Office, Adm 106/2508, No 1036.

98. Deptford Letter Book, 24 December 1742, Public Record Office, Adm 106/3305.

99. Note 27, p47.

100. Navy Board Order to Dockyards, Public Record Office, Adm 106/2511, No 32.

101. Note 19, p240.

102. *Oxford English Dictionary*. This attributes the first use of gig for a boat to John Walcot (Peter Pindar), *Advice to the Future Laureate*, 1790. In the 1812 edition of his *Works*, Vol II, p388.

103. Deptford Letter Book, 11 June 1763, Public Record Office, Adm 106/3260.

104. Note 27. Plate XXIV.

105. Navy Board Order to Dockyards, Public Record Office, Adm 106/2510, No 348.

106. (a) James Stanier Clarke & John M'Arthur, *The Life of Admiral Lord Nelson, KB* (London 1809), Vol II, p282.
(b) Sir Nicholas Harris Nicolas, *Despatches and Letters of Vice Admiral Lord Viscount Nelson* (London 1844), Vol IV, p325.

107. Captain Frederick Marryat, *Frank Mildmay* (London 1829), Ch xi.

108. Note 107, Ch xxiii.

109. Note 107, Ch xxi.

110. Admiral Sir Richard Vesey Hamilton, *Letters and Papers of Admiral of the Fleet Sir Thomas Byam Martin*, Navy Records Society (London 1903), Vol I, p 136.

111. Navy Board Orders to Dockyards, Public Records Office, Adm 106/2512, No 194.

112. Admiralty to Navy Board, Public Record Office, Adm 2/307, p4.

113. *Rate Book for the Valuation of Naval Stores*, 1817.

114. Navy Board Order to Dockyards, Public Record Office, Adm 106/2530, No 166.

115. Note 26, Plate III. Note 27, Plate XXIV.

116. Admiralty to Navy Board, 10 January 1826, Public Record Office, Adm 106/206.

117. Note 81.

118. Navy Board Order to Dockyards, Public Record Office, Adm 106/2509, No 84.

119. Navy Board Orders to Dockyards, Public Record Office, Adm 106/2512, Nos 439, 440 & 441.

120. *Repertory of Arts*, New Series, No LXII. Quoted by Burney, Note 27.

121. Captain Alexander Mackenzie to the Navy Board, 31 December 1820, Public Record Office, Adm 106/1385, M.Off.82.

122. Captain Thomas Wolrige to the Navy Board, 1 January 1823, Public Record Office, Adm 106/1440, WO 79.

123. Captain John Duff Markland to the Navy Board, 1 January 1831, Public Record Office, Adm 106/1391, M Off 177.

124. Captain Maurice Frederick Fitzhardinge Berkeley to Vice-Admiral Charles Elphinstone Fleeming, 5 April 1836, Public Record Office, Adm 1/784, C 209.

125. Captain Thomas White to the Navy Board, 12 March 1822, Public Record Office, Adm 106/1440, C Off 95.

126. Note 74.

127. Admiralty to Navy Board, 29 December 1825, Public Record Office, Adm 106/181.

128. Admiralty to Navy Board, 10 April 1830, Public Record Office, Adm 106/225.

129. Admiralty to Navy Board, 4 March 1831, Public Record Office, Adm 106/231.

130. Public Record Ofice, Index 12171, Section 11A, 1840.

131. Note 130.

132. *Rigging and Seamanship*, 1794, Vol I, p243, quoted by the *Oxford English Dictionary*.

133. Robert Rogers, *Journals of Major Robert Rogers containing an Account of the several Excursions he made under the Generals who commanded upon the continent of North America during the late War* (London 1765), p19.

134. Library of HM Customs and Excise.

135. Note 86.

136. Thomas Pennant, *Journey from London to the Isle of Wight* (London 1787), p171.

137. R H C Gillis, 'The Newquay Pilot Gigs', *Mariner's Mirror* 41 (1955), pp251-255; 'The Pilot Gigs of Cornwall and the Isles of Scilly', *Mariner's Mirror* 55 (1969), pp117- 138.

138. Public Record Office, Index 9294(1), Section 13, 1826.

139. Public Record Office, Index 5074, Section 11A, 1836.

140. Public Record Office, Index 12485, Section 11A, 1860.

141. John M'Neil Boyd, *A Manual for Naval Cadets*, 1st ed (London 1857), p263; 2nd ed (London 1860), p284.

142. *Rate Book for Naval Stores*, 1877.

143. National Maritime Museum, boat draught B (s) i.

144. Public Record Office, Index 12229, Section 11A, 1844.

145. Patent No 1502, dated 2 November 1785.

146. Navy Board to Admiralty, 16 and 25 July 1808, Public Record Office, Adm 106/2244.

147. Navy Board to Admiralty, 4 August 1808, Public Record Office, Adm 106/2244.

148. National Maritime Museum, boat draught Bu(b) 3a.

149. Patent No 1438, dated 18 June 1856.

150. Patent No 3150, dated 23 December 1857.

151. Patent No 3578, dated 17 August 1881.

152. Note 26.

153. National Maritime Museum, draught 7831/63.

154. Public Record Office, Index 21047, Section 11A. 1890

155. National Maritime Museum, draught 7833/63.

156. National Maritime Museum, draughts 7836/63 to 7838/63.

157. National Maritime Museum, draught 7829/63.

158. National Maritime Museum, AGC/xxi.

159. Note 18.

160. Deal Letter Book, 12 February 1761, Public Record Office, Adm 106/3260.

161. Navy Board Order to Dockyards, Public Record Office, Adm 106/2508, No 478.

162. Navy Board Order to Dockyards, Public Record Office, Adm 106/2508, No 579.

163. Navy Board Order to Dockyards, Public Record Office, Adm 106/2514, No 161.

164. Note 141. 1st ed, pp279-281.

165. Public Record Office, Adm 1/5766, 'Admiralty' 29 August 1861; Adm 1/5756, A 2123.

166. Public Record Office, Index 18033, Section 11A, 1868

167. Admiralty to Navy Board, 8 August 1822, Public Record Office, Adm 106/141.

168. Public Record Office, Index 12277, Section 11A, 1847.

169. Public Record Office, Index 12325, Section 11A, 1850.

170. Public Record Office, Index 12549, Section 11A, 1864.

171. Public Record Office, Index 12597, Section 11A, 1867.

172. Public Record Office, Index 18311, Section 11A, 1882.

173. Public Record Office, Index 23956, Section 11A, 1905.

174. Note 15(b), Vol. I, p34.

175. Captain George Anson to Admiralty, 6 January 1737/8, Public Record Office, Adm 1/1439.

176. Navy Board Minutes, 28 September 1742, Public Record Office, Adm 106/2557.

177. Navy Board Orders to Dockyards, PublicRecord Office, Adm 106/2511, No 45.

178. Navy Board Order to Dockyards, Public Record Office, Adm 106/2511. No. 334.

179. Admiralty to Navy Board, 11 August 1823, Public Record Office, Adm 106/153.

180. Navy Board Order to Dockyards, Public Record Office, Adm 106/2522, No 307.

181. Admiralty to Navy Board, 29 November 1828, Public Record Office, Adm 106/216.

182. Public Record Office, Indexes 5074 (1836), 12171 (1840) and 12405 (1855), Section 11A.

183. Note 74.

184. Public Record Office, Indexes 12501 (1861) and 12517 (1862), Section 11A.

185. List of Changes, 529.

186. Admiralty 15 December 1865, Public Record Office, Adm 1/5936.

187. *Gunnery Manual*, 1873.

188. *Notes on Naval Guns*, 1884.

189. *Gunnery Manual*, 1885.

190. *Notes on Naval Guns*, 1889.

191. *Gunnery Manual*, 1892.

192. *Gunnery Manual*, 1901.

193. *Gunnery Manual*, 1907.

194. *Gunnery Manual*, 1868.

INDEX

Page numbers in *italics* refer to illustrations